KU-358-884

Rise and Fall of Incomes Policy

F. W. PAISH

Emeritus Professor of Economics
University of London

Second Edition

Published by

THE INSTITUTE OF ECONOMIC AFFAIRS

1971

First published June 1969
Second Edition July 1971
©
THE INSTITUTE OF ECONOMIC AFFAIRS
1969 and 1971

SBN 255 36016-9

Printed in Great Britain by
THE SOMAN-WHERRY PRESS LTD., NORWICH
Set in Monotype Garamond series 156

PREFACE TO THE FIRST EDITION

The purpose of the *Hobart Papers* is to contribute a stream of authoritative, independent and readable analysis to the discussion of economic opinion and policy. Their general purpose is to appraise the economic framework of laws and institutions in which the deployment of resources most satisfies the preferences of the community as consumers.

Among the many functions of government in the creation of the economic framework is the maintenance of monetary and market institutions that will enable the economy to work without avoidable interruption or congestion. In their failure to master inflation successive British governments have evolved an 'incomes policy' designed to prevent the rise in incomes from outstripping the increase in output.

The growing tendency to blame the failure on the incompetence of the Government, more specifically on its leading Ministers from Mr George Brown to Mr Peter Shore and Mr Wilson, should be muted by the reflection that many of the more articulate economists and most economic journalists in the early 1960s uncritically advocated some variant of 'a wages policy' as a panacea for the central economic debility of slow and uneven growth in output.[1] If the Government deserves special censure, it may be for adopting economic advice that held promise for sanguine political expediency but was only tenuously rooted in economic analysis.

In September 1964, when the incomes policy was in its infancy, the Institute invited Professor F. W. Paish, whose incisive economic analysis of British monetary policy has shed much light on the working of the British economy, to analyse the economics of 'incomes policy' and Mr Jossleyn Hennessy to indicate what

---

[1] One of the first advocates of this approach, as of other discredited policies like a five-year-plan reinforced by direct government intervention in the private sector 'by orders, by threats, by incentives, and by exhortation', was Mr. Andrew Shonfield. Indeed, his Penguin Special, *British Economic Policy since the War* (Penguin Books, 1958), is almost a classic statement of the policies that became fashionable among journalists and economic publicists in the period leading to devaluation in 1967.

lessons, if any, could be learned from attempts to operate 'incomes policy' on the Continent. Their two texts were published as Hobart Paper 29, *Policy for Incomes?*. In the last five years 'incomes policy' has had a chequered career that has finally ended in all but generally recognised failure: only politicians and Mr Aubrey Jones, and others whose intellectual reputations are at stake, refuse to confess defeat. Although it may have dammed an increase in incomes in an industry or a group of industries for a time, it has patently failed to prevent inflation; it has diverted attention from the fundamental changes in the British economy that should have been undertaken and that would have had to be undertaken if it had not had such a long trial; and it has created new stresses and strains that would have been avoided if it had not been introduced or if it had been abandoned as soon as its failure had become apparent. In this period Professor Paish and Mr Hennessy revised their texts for second, third and fourth editions in October 1966, February 1967 and October 1968.

The economic discussion of 'incomes policy' has now changed from its merits, which are seen to be few, and its demerits, which are more obvious, to the reasons for its failure and the extent to which statistics record its unhappy history. In considering a further publication on the subject, the Institute decided that the time had come to complement Hobart Paper 29 with a second Hobart Paper that would examine the newer issues as they had evolved in the five years since 1964. Professor Paish has written an almost entirely new text, for which only the early few pages of Hobart Paper 29 have been adapted. In it he closely examines the statistical evidence on wage rates, earnings, the wage trend, output per man-hour, productivity and productive potential, income from employment, unemployment and unused productive potential, personal incomes and consumption, the balance of payments and stock accumulation, labour costs and export prices, and the terms of trade.

Professor Paish's close analysis of the recent economic history also provides an incisive commentary on government policy and the power of trade unions in conditions of high employment, and also material for judging the likely trend of economic events in the home economy and in the balance of payments with other countries. He concludes that the required surplus on overseas

[4]

account to finance current trade and repay debts is unlikely to be reached by 1969 and that the desired target of a £500 million surplus is unlikely to be reached until the second half of 1971 at the earliest. He judges that, even if increasing confidence in sterling lessens the desire of external creditors for repayment of debt, it would be necessary to maintain a surplus of £300 million a year or more. This aim, he argues, implies that incomes must 'never again' be allowed to rise as fast relatively to output as in the last few years; and this, in turn, that the margin of unused productive resources and the average level of unemployment must be higher than it has been since the end of the war.

These will be regarded as unwelcome conclusions from a rigorous analysis. They arise not from the dismal science of economics but from the application of its logic to the political failures of government since the early 1960s. The unpalatable truth will have to be faced sooner rather than later that incomes policy is no more likely to be effective if government cannot prevent inflation than sitting on the safety valve of a well-stoked steam engine is likely to prevent the escape of steam. If the economy had been made more mobile and flexible by removing the elements of monopoly in industry and the trade unions, it might have been possible to avoid serious inflation with unemployment as low as 2 per cent, although even that would be difficult in an economy that requires to be responsive to changes in international supply and demand. But recent British governments have done very little to make the economy sufficiently adaptable; instead of removing obstacles to movement—restrictive practices, rent restrictions, ploughing back profits, the disincentives to saving, the agglomerations of labour and capital in nationalised industry, subsidies to the inefficient and out-dated, high taxation, and import restrictions—it has had to resort to the doubtful expedient of resisting increases in incomes by persuasion and law. Its failure could have been, and was, foreseen before it was introduced, but the 'fair-minded' pragmatic British might not have been convinced until it was tried. Five years may be long enough, and the present Government has at long last had to turn to reform the powers of the trade unions. But even that will not be sufficient if the other impediments to the free movement of labour and capital are allowed to remain undisturbed.

The Institute, like its Advisory Council, does not necessarily share Professor Paish's analysis or conclusions, but it is glad to offer his new Hobart Paper to complement the first as a further instalment of an economic analysis that shows how government policy has failed, what its consequences are likely to be, and what they might have been had governments heeded better advice in time.

May 1969   EDITOR

PREFACE TO THE SECOND EDITION

Since the First Edition in June 1969 an important change, Professor Paish argues, has taken place in the labour market and the financial situation of the economy. 'Demand pull' (basically monetary inflation) has in the main been replaced by 'cost push' (basically trade union monopoly power) as the cause of most of the accelerated inflation in 1970 and 1971.

Professor Paish surveys the main economic developments since 1969 in some detail, and back to 1963 in more general outline. He reviews the economic policies that could deal with inflation and finds that they are mostly too slow or 'unpleasant'. He concludes that the Government is right to postpone them as long as possible and that, if there is 'no clear evidence of a substantial slowing down of the rise in employment incomes by towards the end of the year, it will have to consider what more positive action it can take', by which he means 'more direct government action to restrain the rate of income rise', or in more popular language a 'wage freeze'.

Professor Paish emphasises that his proposal does not conflict with the analysis in the First Edition (or in the earlier *Hobart Paper* 29) which led him to oppose the 'incomes policy' then widely supported. He says there was no objection to the *purpose* of restraint on increases in wage rates, but that in conditions of demand pull it would have been unnecessary or ineffective. It is now more likely to be effective because the conditions have changed to cost push.

Professor Paish's *Postscript* raises or provokes a number of fundamental questions in economic theory and applied economics

[6]

arising directly or indirectly out of the many aspects on which it touches: inflation, trade union power in the labour market, real and money wages before and after tax (and other deductions), control of consumption by monetary supply, the optimum amounts or rates of unemployment and liquidation, the optimum combination of long-term and short-term measures in mastering inflation, the administrative efficacy of 'wage freeze', the exchange rates and others.

Is it chance that wage inflation has been experienced in several Western countries since 1969? Are the reasons for it common or do they differ?

As trade unions have had legalised monopoly power since (and before) the war, was it the failure of 'incomes policy' in 1969 that induced them to use it for the first time in 1969? Why did they not use it earlier?

Since an important reason lies in the growing awareness of the erosion of real wages by rising taxation and increasing national insurance deductions in the previous three or four years, is it not here that government policy should be reconsidered?

May a further reason be the gradual awakening to continuing inflation that the unions saw they could incorporate as a bargaining counter in asking for wages to cover not merely *past* but also *future* inflation?

Has increasing taxation (including social insurance) lost its power to restrain consumption? May it *intensify* inflation by reducing 'take-home' pay and inciting wage demands when 'social wages' are not seen, or not valued, as a part of income?

If consumption cannot be restrained politically by control of the money supply because of unemployment and liquidations, what is the optimum amount of unused or reserve resources of labour and capital in an economy which exports a fifth of its national product to pay for imports and has to adapt itself to changes in world conditions of supply and demand?

If the unemployed capable of re-employment are re-trained for new or growing industries, is it 'politically impossible' for governments to explain that the economy may in some periods require a reserve of perhaps 4 or 5 per cent unemployed (including 1 per cent 'unemployable'), with 95 or 96 out of 100 in continuing work?

Has inflation as a means of maintaining high employment lost its potency? Must it be replaced by a *rising* rate of inflation? Has the 'snowball' effect of discounted inflation been under-estimated?

Why have governments not been more resolute in acting on the three types of demand that Professor Paish explains could have been restrained—personal consumption, public expenditure, private investment? Have they *correctly* judged the technical, administrative or political probabilities?

If consumption cannot be restrained by increases in taxation, how far might it be restrained by charging for government goods and services which would not reduce 'take-home' pay, and thus help to restrain wage demands and intensify incentives to increase earnings?

May *long*-term measures—reduction of labour monopoly, reduction of government expenditure, increase in competitiveness, etc.—create a public sentiment in favour of government policies to master inflation that will make them politically easier in the *short* run?

If the requirement is a short-term expedient, is the time-scale of direct control by wage-squeeze shorter than the six months thought to make reduction in the supply of money effective?

May better monetary control be made possible by reducing or withdrawing unemployment benefits or social benefits from the unemployed or strikers? How can the innocent or deserving be distinguished?

Would monetary policy be further strengthened by making the economy more competitive, so making it difficult for employers to pass on inflationary wage increases to the consumer?

Since the efforts of 'incomes policies' up to 1969 have had very small effect in restraining incomes, would a wages freeze in 1971 restrain them any more if the unions could evade it easily by reclassifying labour categories to justify higher wage-rates, demanding fringe benefits, etc.?

Does the emphasis on employment in general or national totals of unemployment, incomes, consumption, prices, etc., distract attention from relative price movements that may be relevant for the explanation of economic events and the more efficient working of the economy?

[8]

These and other long-term and short-term issues are raised in considering how the British economy can be freed from the inflation that has debilitated it since the war. Economists differ widely on them, and Professor Paish will not agree on many, or most. In the last resort the use, extent and timing of a 'freeze' as a temporary expedient is a matter of practical judgement and political assessment as well as of economic theory and statistical analysis of short-period movements in national output, prices, wages (and other) costs, unemployment, etc. But Professor Paish's *Postscript* will clarify the difficulties economists find in analysing the causes of inflation and governments in making the choice between the most desirable and the most convenient cures.

May 1971   EDITOR

THE AUTHOR

FRANK PAISH was born in January 1898. Eldest son of Sir George Paish, he was educated at Winchester College and Trinity College, Cambridge. Employed by Standard Bank of South Africa, 1921–32. Lecturer at London School of Economics, 1932–8; Reader 1938–49; Professor of Economics with special reference to Business Finance from 1949 to 1965. Deputy-Director of Programmes, Ministry of Aircraft Production, 1941–5. Author of *Insurance Funds and their Investment* (with G. L. Schwartz), 1934; *The Postwar Financial Problem and Other Essays*, 1950; *Business Finance*, 1953; *Studies in an Inflationary Economy*, 1962; *How the Economy Works, and Other Essays*, 1970.

[9]

CONTENTS

TABLES

CHARTS

I. INTRODUCTION

Many differences of opinion on matters of economic policy are caused by disagreements about the relative importance of ultimate ends. Thus, those for whom increased equality of incomes is more important than a faster reduction of poverty achieved through more rapid growth of national product will naturally disagree with those who would give first priority to growth. And those who believe that extreme full employment is desirable, not only for its own sake but also because they think that rapid growth is possible only with some degree of inflation, will differ from those who believe that inflation is not only grossly unjust in its effects but also leads to the inefficient use of resources and the survival of inefficient managements, and thus in the long run tends to slow down growth.

The difference of opinion analysed in this *Hobart Paper* is, however, not of this sort. In this discussion both sides agree in giving first priority to the prevention of inflation, that is to say, to preventing rises in money incomes from outstripping the sustainable growth of output. We can therefore say that both sides agree on the necessity of an 'incomes policy': where they disagree is about the way in which it can be carried out. One side believes that its common objective can best be achieved by inducing or compelling trade unions and employers' organisations to limit rises in wages and profits to rates which are compatible with the growth of output and with long-term price stability. The other holds the view that such a limitation, even if achieved, would be ineffective so long as there was an excess demand for labour and unnecessary if there were not. It believes that the only way to prevent wages and other incomes from rising too fast is to prevent the emergence of an excess demand for goods and services and an excess demand for labour. This requirement implies a level of unemployment as high as would be consistent with the absence of inflation with a fully competitive labour market. In this *Paper* the attempt is made to examine the assumptions which lie behind the two views and to see how far they can be reconciled.

[13]

II. INFLATION

Causes of inflation

One, though not the only, cause of the disagreement is a conflict of opinion about the ways in which an inflation can start. Both sides agree that an inflation *can* be generated by an excessive rise in the demand for goods and services, whether by public authorities or by the private sector. This is the so-called 'demand inflation'. Where they disagree is on whether inflation can also be initiated by an excessive rise in wage rates forced on reluctant employers by the use of monopoly power by the trade unions. This is the so-called 'cost inflation'.

The way in which cost inflation is supposed to operate seems simple. Employers are forced by trade union pressure to grant increases in wage rates in excess of the rise in output per head. To maintain profit margins, employers are forced to increase prices. Their higher wages enable consumers to buy as much as before, in spite of the higher prices, while the increase in prices induces further demands by the unions—and so *ad infinitum*. If this view is accepted it follows that, if trade unions can be persuaded not to press claims for excessive wage increases, a cost inflation can be prevented from starting, and can be arrested even after it has begun.

This apparently simple description of a cost inflation, however, conceals some implicit assumptions which are by no means obviously true. First, if an inflation is to be *initiated* by rising costs, it must start from a condition where there is no excess demand—that is to say, a condition in which output is rising by no more than its sustainable rate of growth and incomes are rising no faster than output. In such conditions, no employer under pressure to grant an increase in wages larger than the expected increase in output per head can expect in advance to be able to pass on his higher costs in the form of higher prices without losing sales. He will therefore do his best to resist the demand, even at the risk of a strike, and if he is forced to accept it will consider that some marginal activity, either existing or projected, has been made unprofitable. He will therefore reduce his output and his demand for labour, or, more probably in a growing economy with a rising working population, will not increase them as much as he would otherwise have done. He will also tend to restrict his plans for new investment below what they would otherwise have been, thus causing demand for investment goods to be less than expected and intensifying the effects on the profits of investment goods industries of their own wage increases. The higher wages, even if general, are thus achieved only at the cost of lower business profits and rising unemployment. Only if employers confidently expect that they will be able to pass on their higher costs in higher prices without losing sales will they maintain their output and demand for labour at the levels at which they would have stood but for the excessive increases in wages. Excessive wage demands will therefore be granted without rising unemployment *only if inflation is already expected*. 'Cost inflation' thus becomes the way in which inflations are perpetuated rather than initiated.

Inflation and the money supply

Second, even when an inflation is in progress, a further assumption is necessary to enable a cost inflation to continue indefinitely. Each rise in money incomes will require the holding of more money to finance consumption, while each rise in prices of physical assets, and of titles to their ownership, will require additional money to be held for financing investment. If the total quantity of money is not rising, or rising only as fast as real output, money will have to be withdrawn from idle balances in order to increase the average velocity of circulation, and this will be accompanied by a rise in interest rates.[1] As the excessively rapid rise of incomes proceeds, the velocity of circulation must continue to increase, and rates of interest will continue to rise until they reach a level which checks the rise in investment and reduces the demand for labour. It is true that if the economy starts from a condition of high liquidity and low interest rates, such as existed in 1946, the process may continue for a long time before it is checked; but to make any inflation truly self-perpetuating requires a suitably expansionary monetary policy.

The checking of an inflation through a shortage of money, often slow, can of course be speeded up by government fiscal policy. If part of the money flow can be diverted, so that it ceases to create increased incomes on its next circuit, the rise in incomes

[1] For a discussion of the relationship between changes in national money income, the quantity of money and the rate of interest, see Paish, *Studies in an Inflationary Economy*, Macmillan, 1962, Chapter I, p. 3, and *Long-term and Short-term Interest Rates*, Manchester University Press, 1966, Chapter 3.

can be directly prevented from perpetuating itself. Such a policy is effective even though it is implemented by a rise in indirect taxes, of which the impact effect is to raise prices further. Unlike higher prices received by producers, the proceeds of which are paid out in increased wages or dividends or used to finance increased investment, a rise in prices due to higher indirect taxes is not self-perpetuating, *provided the government does not use the proceeds to increase its income-creating expenditure.* The effects of a larger budget surplus will be particularly marked if the increase is used to repay short-term government debt to the banks, thus reducing their liquid assets ratio and accelerating the rise in interest rates.

Trade unions as monopolists of labour

The case for a policy of attempting to induce the unions to refrain from pressing for wage increases in excess of the rise in output per head does not, however, depend only on a belief in the existence of cost inflation. Even if we believe that, in the absence of demand inflation, the unions cannot enforce excessive increases in wages without causing a rise in unemployment, there is still a strong case for trying to persuade them to limit wage increases to amounts which can be paid without either raising unemployment or raising prices. It pays a monopolist to raise his prices even at the cost of some reduction in the volume of his sales, and if the unions are in practice effective monopolists of the supply of labour, the same will be true of them.

When only a *minority* of occupations is effectively unionised, their unions can raise wages above the level at which they would stand in a fully competitive labour market at the cost of some reduction in the number employed in those occupations. They can do this without raising the general level of unemployment provided that people who are prevented from working in the unionised occupations are able to obtain employment in non-unionised occupations, thus driving wages there down below what they would have been in a fully competitive system. If, however, *all* occupations are strongly unionised, the general level of real wages can be kept above its competitive level only by forcing some potential workers out of employment altogether. It is possible, with suitable assumptions, to construct hypothetical cases where the combination of strong and ruthless unions with a government determined to prevent inflation at any cost will result in an unemployment level of 5 per cent, or even 10 per cent.[1] On such assumptions those still employed would obtain so much larger a share of the national product, at the cost partly of people rendered unemployed and partly of profits, that the rise in the size of their share would more than offset the fall in the size of the product, so that, at least in the short run, they would be better off. Whether they would be better off also in the long run depends on what assumptions we make about the effects on the rate of growth of output.

It is probable, of course, that long before unemployment had reached the levels which, on these assumptions, would be needed to reconcile the unions' policies with the absence of inflation, the government would find the rise politically intolerable. If they could not induce the unions to change their policies, the government would be forced to seek a cure for the unemployment by increasing its expenditure or reducing taxes, thus expanding demand and profits, and at the same time raising prices and depriving union members already in employment of part of the rise in real wages which their rise in money wages would otherwise have brought them. This loss of real income would no doubt bring increased union pressure for wage increases and new measures to expand demand, and so on. In this sense it is perhaps possible to speak of a self-perpetuating 'cost-push' inflation.

III. APPROPRIATE AND INAPPROPRIATE 'INCOMES POLICIES'

Control of wages

If it could be shown that in practice there existed conditions in which the trade unions were able and willing, even in the absence of demand inflation, to force wage rates up well above the level which would have existed in a competitive labour market, there would be every argument for the government to try to escape from the choice between inflation and a high level of unemployment by attempting to induce or compel the unions to abandon this use of their monopoly power. If the arguments in favour of a 'wages policy' were based on the need to escape from such a

[1] C. D. Finch, *Some Problems of Wages Policy* (unpublished London University Ph.D. Thesis), University of London Library.

dilemma, the discussion would turn merely on whether the unions, in that economy at that time, were in practice able and willing to hold the rest of the community up to ransom in this way. Once the facts were ascertained, there could be no further argument about the desirability of a 'wages policy', though there could, of course, be differences of opinion about methods of implementation. These would no doubt depend largely on how much the activities of the trade unions were thought to be adding to the cost, in terms of unemployment, of preventing inflation. If it could be shown that this cost was anything like the theoretically possible 5 per cent or more, public opinion would probably support a revision of trade union law,[1] while if the additional unemployment were shown to be relatively small, the support for a revision of the law would be correspondingly less, and the methods used to implement a wages policy would probably continue mainly to be limited to attempts at persuasion.

It would, however, seem that some advocates of a 'wages policy' go further than this and wish, not only to prevent the level of unemployment (consistent with the absence of inflation) from being forced above what it would have been in a competitive labour market, but also to hold down the levels of wages and of unemployment below their competitive equilibrium levels. The desirability of such a policy is doubtful, its practicability more than doubtful. If it could be implemented, its effects would be identical with those of an employers' monopoly designed to keep wage rates down below their competitive level, and therefore the exact opposite of the effects of a trade union monopoly designed to keep wages above their competitive level. People already employed would lose part of the wage increases they would otherwise have received, there would be less unemployment, and profits would increase.

(i) Desirability
On the credit side of such a policy can be set a fall in unemployment which, if the policy could be really effectively enforced, might be to an extremely low level. In addition, a fringe of

[1] An approach towards such a policy has recently been made by the publication of the White Paper *In Place of Strife* (Cmnd. 3888, January 1969), and by the proposal to introduce a bill into Parliament to implement some of its recommendations. While the approach has so far been tentative, it has aroused strong opposition from many trade unions and its effective implementation is doubtful. It may, however, provide a precedent for stronger measures later.

workers, who would otherwise not have taken paid employment at all, may be recruited, often on a part-time basis, to help meet the excessive demand for labour. Thus output, in the short run, would be higher than it would have been with a competitive labour market. At the same time there would be rises in retained profits, very possibly in tax yields and in the government's budget surplus, and possibly also in personal saving, if the increase in the savings of those receiving higher dividends more than offset the fall in the savings of those receiving lower wages and salaries. Thus it is likely that total saving would rise, and with it total investment, so that there might be a tendency not only for current output to be higher but also for it to grow faster.

On the debit side can be set, not only the lower real incomes and standards of living of the bulk of the population, but also some loss of dynamism in the economy. In conditions in which wage rates are held artificially low and profits artificially high, it is easy for even inefficient managements to stay in business. The pressure for improved efficiency would thus be relaxed, and it is possible that, in spite of the higher rates of saving and investment, in the long run the rate of growth might be slower than in an economy where efficiency was enforced by competition.

(ii) Feasibility

Of more practical importance than the desirability of such a policy is its feasibility. The difficulties of its inauguration are largely political, while those of its subsequent maintenance are mainly economic. The most obvious difficulty is to persuade the unions to agree to collaborate in keeping wages below the levels at which they would have stood in a competitive labour market. The only argument likely to have any effect in persuading them to accept such a policy is that this is the only way in which unemployment can be kept at an extremely low level without inflation. From the unions' point of view, the chief argument against it is that it would not only keep down wages but also increase profits; and it is likely that, in trying to meet this objection, the government will offer measures, especially in the form of profit and price controls, which reduce the advantages and increase the disadvantages of the policy itself.

[19]

There is no need to consider in detail proposals for the direct limitation of profits. To try to peg profit margins would mean that every firm would be working on a cost-plus basis and would lose all incentive to keep down costs. To attempt to fix all prices at levels which, given the agreed rates of wages, would give normal profits to the reasonably efficient firm would, perhaps, be slightly less impracticable; but if the attempt were successful it would frustrate the whole purpose of the operation. Unemployment can be kept abnormally low only by keeping the demand for labour abnormally high; and the demand for labour can be kept abnormally high only by keeping the employment of labour abnormally profitable. If profits are held down to the same level as would obtain with a competitive labour market, the demand for labour will be correspondingly restrained and unemployment will not fall.

It is more probable that the unions would be offered an agreement whereby, though profits would be allowed to rise, the extra profits would be removed by increased taxation. Such a policy, while technically enforceable, would add substantially to the debit side of a wages policy. A high rate of profits tax has no effect on the inefficient firm which is only just managing to stay in business, while it increases the difficulty of efficient firms in obtaining the finance they need for expansion, both from internal sources and, very probably, in the market. It also reduces the incentive to keep down costs, especially in the form of expenditures such as advertising, which may still be yielding some residual benefit to the firm after the tax, it may be hoped, is reduced or removed. No system could be better designed to slow down growth than one which keeps the inefficient alive, prevents the efficient from expanding, and reduces for everyone the incentive to keep down costs.

Alternatively, the government might offer, as an inducement to the unions, higher taxation, not of all profits but of distributed profits only. Such a measure, while avoiding some of the disadvantages of heavy taxation of all profits, introduces some new ones of its own. A system of heavier taxes on distributed than on retained profits causes few problems for the well-established but slowly-growing company, which is able to finance its capital requirements entirely out of its own resources, but makes it more expensive, and probably more difficult, for a fast-growing company, which needs more capital than it can save, to raise new capital in the market. It also tends to induce companies which are growing little if at all to retain profits for which they have no real use. It thus tends to cause capital to be used for less productive rather than more productive purposes.[1]

Difficulties of enforcement

Even if the political difficulties of obtaining the agreement of the trade unions could be overcome, it is unlikely that a wages policy would be successful for long in holding wages and unemployment below their competitive equilibrium levels. As time went on, the administration of the policy would encounter increasing difficulties. These would arise basically because an attempt was being made to hold wages below the level which would equate the demand for labour with the supply. Although such a policy might be effective for a limited period of emergency, an attempt to maintain it permanently would face the employers, the trade unions and probably also the government with difficulties so acute that they would lead ultimately to its breakdown.

With the demand for labour in excess of the supply at the price, many employers will find themselves with plant and equipment they cannot man, and profitable orders they cannot fulfil, for lack of labour. In these conditions it is extremely difficult, even by penal legislation, to prevent employers from attempting to attract the labour they need by methods which raise their labour costs. Even if standard wage-rates can be effectively controlled, the other methods of offering higher remuneration, in cash or kind, are innumerable: guaranteed overtime; upgrading; piece rates; merit payments; bonus or incentive schemes; profit sharing; pension schemes and other fringe benefits; even improved canteen and other amenities. All these methods (however desirable some of them may be in themselves) add to labour costs, and to the real, even if not the money incomes, of employees; and all are means of bidding up the price of labour, the excess of which over standard wage rates is likely to become increasingly apparent the longer the wages policy is maintained.

[1] Both these fears have been realised in recent years by the introduction, with effect from 1966, of corporation tax, which causes distributed profits to be taxed much more heavily than retained profits, and by subsequent increases in its rate, which have raised the taxation of all profits.

The only effective way yet found to stop such a 'wage drift' is to have a firm agreement between employers for allocating scarce labour, so that they may no longer bid for labour in the market but must draw it from a central pool, sharing the labour shortages on some agreed basis. A scheme of this sort has been successfully operated for many years by the South African mining industry, with the object and result of keeping African wages below the level at which they would have stood if the mines had competed freely with each other for African labour. But it is difficult to believe that a scheme of this sort could be successfully established in this country.

Just as the employers' associations would find it increasingly difficult to ensure that their members kept the spirit, as well as the letter, of the agreement, so the trade unions would find it increasingly difficult to prevent their members from taking unofficial action to secure wage increases larger than provided for. As time went on, the unions would find their branches and members increasingly out of sympathy with headquarters; the influence of shop stewards would grow at the expense of the union officials; unofficial strikes and other means of bringing pressure on employers would become increasingly common; breakaway unions would be formed with increasing frequency; and finally, unless the agreement had already broken down as the result of breaches by employers, the unions would be faced with the choice of abandoning the agreement or losing all control over their members.

The government's difficulties, apart from those caused by unofficial strikes and by the threat of inflation as the agreement gradually collapsed, would arise largely from the need they would feel to set a good example to employers in the private sector, by keeping the agreement strictly in negotiations with their own employees and by trying to insist that local authorities and the managements of nationalised industries did the same. Consequently, as the agreement broke down in the private sector, employees' earnings in the public sector would tend to fall increasingly behind. The result would be not only unofficial strikes and other labour troubles, frequently in occupations where they would cause the maximum of inconvenience to the public, but also an increasing inability to recruit and retain labour for the public service in the numbers and of the quality required.

This would be the more disastrous in that most of the really essential public services are now under the control of public authorities.

IV. THE EXTENT OF UNEMPLOYMENT

Even if we accept that, while there is every justification for trying to dissuade trade unions from using their monopoly power to force wage increases larger than would have been consistent with the absence of inflation in a competitive labour market, an attempt to keep wage increases below the equilibrium competitive level is of doubtful desirability and unlikely to succeed for long, we still need the answers to three further questions before we can formulate a practical policy:

first, what, in the existing situation, is the minimum level of unemployment consistent with the absence of inflation? (pp. 23–47).

second, what would that level be with a competitive labour market? (pp. 47–51).

third, how effective can we expect a policy of income restraint to be in closing the gap between the two? (pp. 51–60).

If the existing minimum level of unemployment were found to be substantially higher than the competitive level, it would imply that the unions were exercising considerable monopoly power, and that there would be a strong case for a wages policy; if, on the other hand, the difference were found to be small, the case for a wages policy would be correspondingly less strong. In no case, however, would an attempt be justified to keep wage increases and unemployment below the levels which would have existed in a non-inflationary competitive market.

How much unemployment to prevent inflation?

There is considerable evidence about the levels of unemployment which in the past have accompanied various rates of inflation. To measure them we first of all have to decide on a suitable measure of inflation. To define inflation merely in terms of the rate of rise in prices, while broadly valid for large and prolonged changes, is not adequate for the relatively small and short-period movements with which we shall be mainly concerned. Market

[23]

prices are affected by changes in indirect taxation, while factor cost prices are affected by changes in import prices which, if accompanied by similar changes in export prices, do not affect the real national income. A better definition of inflation is that it is a condition in which money incomes are rising faster than the flow of goods and services on which to spend them—that is to say, faster than real national income. But this definition is also not adequate, for an accelerated rise of money incomes may be accompanied for a time by an equally rapid rise of output and real income, achieved by a higher level of employment.[1] But while the rise of incomes can continue indefinitely, and indeed is likely to accelerate as unemployment falls, the rapid rise of output can be maintained only until full employment is reached, and must then slow down to equality with the long-term trend of growth. The inflation, already implicit in the rapid rise of incomes, now comes into the open. The definition of inflation must therefore be a condition in which incomes are rising faster, not than the current rise in real national income, but than the *maintainable* rise. Apart from the effects of changes in the terms of trade and in net income from foreign investments, this is the same thing as the maintainable rise of output, or, as it is sometimes called, the rise of productive potential.

In current discussion of the rate of rise of incomes, attention is often concentrated on rises in nationally negotiated wage rates. The index of weekly wage rates has the advantage of prompt publication, but as an indication of income change it suffers from two disadvantages. One is that at certain periods wage increases have taken the form not only of rises in weekly rates but also of a reduction in the number of hours worked to earn them. Since 1958 the length of the standard working week has fallen by over 9 per cent, of which about half has been reflected in a fall in the number of hours worked, the remainder representing a rise in hours worked at overtime rates.

We can partly overcome the difficulty of changes in the length of the working week by using hourly, rather than weekly, wage rates, but the other objection to the use of the index of wage rates is more serious. There are times when changes in weekly,

---

[1] For fuller descriptions of this process, see Paish, 'Inflation and the Balance of Payments', *Scottish Journal of Political Economy*, November 1968, pp. 216–222; and 'How the Economy Works', *Lloyds Bank Review*, April 1968, pp. 5–8.

or even hourly, wage rates bear little relationship to changes in pay received. To some extent this is due to changes in the amount of overtime worked; but, even apart from this, there are times when hourly earnings rise much faster than hourly wage rates. This difference is known as 'wage drift', official estimates of which are shown in Table I.

TABLE I
WAGE RATES, EARNINGS AND WAGE-DRIFT:
ALL MANUAL WORKERS, 1956–68

		Unemployment (% in GB)	Average hourly wage rates	Average hourly earnings (excluding effects of overtime)	'Wage drift'
				(Percentage change compared with corresponding month of previous year)	
1956	Apr.	1·2	+8·3	+9·3	+1·0
	Oct.	1·2	+7·6	+8·2	+0·6
1957	Apr.	1·6	+2·5	+3·8	+1·3
	Oct.	1·3	+5·6	+6·6	+1·0
1958	Apr.	2·0	+4·8	+5·9	+1·1
	Oct.	2·4	+3·7	+3·4	—0·3
1959	Apr.	2·4	+3·5	+3·5	+0·0
	Oct.	1·9	+1·4	+2·9	+1·5
1960	Apr.	1·8	+4·4	+6·4	+2·0
	Oct.	1·5	+5·5	+7·3	+1·8
1961	Apr.	1·5	+6·2	+6·5	+0·3
	Oct.	1·6	+6·4	+6·9	+0·5
1962	Apr.	1·9	+4·1	+5·2	+1·1
	Oct.	2·2	+4·2	+4·4	+0·2
1963	Apr.	2·6	+3·6	+4·0	+0·4
	Oct.	2·1	+2·3	+3·6	+1·3
1964	Apr.	1·8	+4·9	+6·5	+1·6
	Oct.	1·5	+5·7	+8·1	+2·4
1965	Apr.	1·5	+5·3	+8·0	+2·7
	Oct.	1·4	+7·3	+9·5	+2·2
1966	Apr.	1·3	+8·0	+9·7	+1·7
	Oct.	1·9	+5·6	+6·5	+0·9
1967	Apr.	2·4	+2·7	+3·0	+0·3
	Oct.	2·4	+5·3	+5·0	—0·3
1968	Apr.	2·5	+8·6	+7·7	—0·9
	Oct.	2·4	+6·0	+6·9	+0·9

Source: The source of Cols. 2 to 4 is Table B.15 of the March, 1969 issue of *Statistics on Incomes, Prices, Employment and Production.* The negative wage drift in April 1968 was due mainly to special factors.

[25]

The figures of Table I have been used for the construction of Chart 1, with the mid-points of the annual increases in wage-rates and earnings coinciding in time with the unemployment percentages.

Two main conclusions can be drawn from the Table and Chart. The first is that there is a clear tendency for both wage-rates and earnings to rise faster when unemployment is low, as in 1955–56, 1960–61 and 1964–66, than when it is relatively high, as in 1958–59, 1962–63 and 1967. The anomalous effects for 1966–68 resulting from the 'wage-freeze' imposed in the second half of 1966 will be discussed in a later section (pp. 51–60). And the second is that the faster rise in earnings than in wage-rates is significant only in years of low unemployment; in years of high unemployment 'wage-drift' is small or may even be negative. The rate of rise of earnings therefore fluctuates more widely than that of wage-rates. Since it is wage-rates, rather than earnings, which are determined by bargaining between trade unions and employers' organisations, it is for those who believe that excessive increases in earned incomes are caused by trade union pressure (cost-push inflation), rather than by an excessive demand for labour (demand-pull inflation), to explain both how it is that trade union pressure becomes effective only when unemployment is low and also why it is only at such times that 'wage-drift' occurs.

From an inspection of Chart 1, it would appear that, at one extreme, an unemployment level of about 1·3 per cent is accompanied by a rise in hourly earnings of 9 per cent or more, while at the other an unemployment level of about 2·4 per cent is accompanied by an earnings rise of only 3 to 4 per cent. Thus a decrease of about 1·1 per cent in unemployment is accompanied by a rise of about 5·5 per cent in earnings, an inverse ratio of about 5 to 1. If, however, we attempt to apply a scale constructed on this ratio to all the data, we find that while in most years there is fairly good agreement, there are also a number of discrepancies (in addition to that in 1967–68, noted above), particularly in the early stages of a change of trend. Indeed, there are years (1957, 1960 and 1966) when earnings move in the same direction as unemployment, instead of inversely.

These discrepancies seem to arise mainly because unemployment is not always a good indicator of changes in demand, chiefly because changes in unemployment frequently, although not

[26]

invariably, lag appreciably behind changes in output or, more strictly, behind changes in the relationship between output and productive potential. It is changes in this relationship which seem to provide the best indicator of changes in the pressure of demand against which to measure changes in the level of earned incomes. We shall also relate it to changes in the percentage of unemployment, with and without a time-lag.

Productive potential

Productive potential may be defined as the physical limit to the amount which could be produced in an economy, whatever the level of demand, given existing resources, abilities, organisation, institutions, habits, tastes and prejudices. This physical limit fortunately rises from year to year. Its rate of increase depends on three factors: the rate of increase of output per man-hour, which (apart from cyclical factors) is brought about mainly by a combination of improvements in the techniques of production and management with an increasing quantity of capital; the increase, if any, in the number at work; and the change, if any, in the average number of hours worked a year. All three factors fluctuate cyclically, with changes in the level of demand. Output per man-hour is probably also affected by changes in the number of hours worked per week, rising as the length of the working week falls, though not by enough, at the present number of hours, to prevent a net loss of output. For the purpose of the present calculation, it is assumed that a fall of 1 per cent in the number of hours worked raises output per man-hour by 0·4 per cent and reduces output (below what it would otherwise have been) by 0·6 per cent.

As well as fluctuating cyclically, the number of hours worked a week has tended to fall, mainly since 1959, although only about half as fast as the standard hours fixed by agreement between employers and unions, the difference being made up by an increase in the number of hours worked at overtime rates. This fall in hours has tended to slow down the rise of productive potential. On the other hand, the upward trend in the number at work has until recently helped to accelerate the rise in productive potential. Since 1966, however, the accident of the age distribution of the population has temporarily checked this rise, which is not likely to be resumed until towards the mid-1970s.

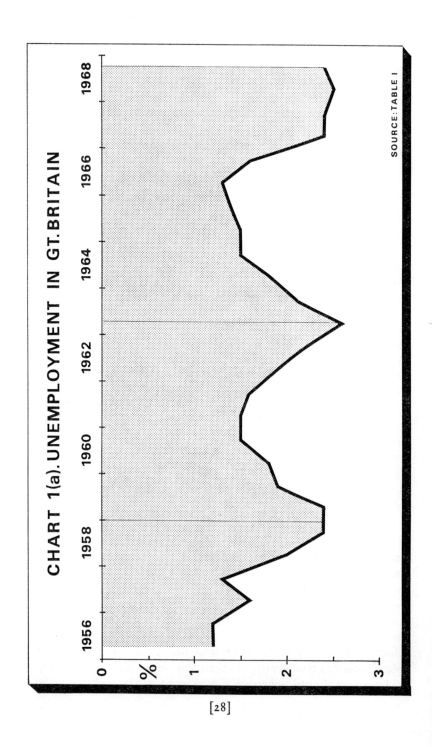

CHART 1(a). UNEMPLOYMENT IN GT.BRITAIN

SOURCE: TABLE I

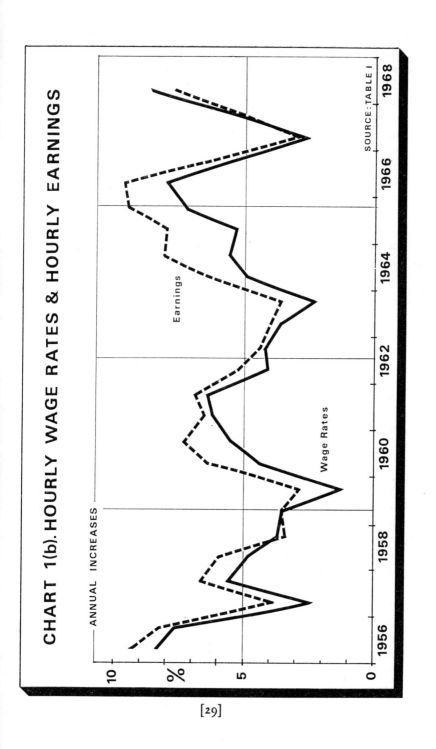

CHART 1(b). HOURLY WAGE RATES & HOURLY EARNINGS

ANNUAL INCREASES

%

10

5

0

1956   1958   1960   1962   1964   1966   1968

Earnings

Wage Rates

SOURCE: TABLE I

[29]

To eliminate the effects of cyclical changes in all three factors, we calculate their changes between periods at similar stages of different business cycles, in which the pressure of demand is judged to be similar. Three such periods are the second quarters of 1952, 1959 and 1963. All three were periods of fairly high unemployment, just at the beginning of the upturns of output which inaugurated the new cycles. We cannot, however, make similar use of the second quarter of 1968, although unemployment was at almost exactly the same level as in the second quarter of 1963, because in it output was checked by a sharply disinflationary budget, whereas in 1963 it was encouraged by an expansionary one. Fortunately, however, we can make a valid comparison between the last quarter of 1962 and the last quarter of 1967. The increases in output per man-hour during these periods are shown in Table II.

TABLE II

INCREASES IN OUTPUT PER MAN-HOUR, 1952–67

Year and Quarter	Percentage unemployed	Employment	Hours worked	Man-hours worked	output	Output per man-hour
			(Average 1958 = 100)			
1952—II	2·21	97·1	98·9	96·0	86·2	89·8
1959—II	2·17	100·4	100·7	101·1	103·8	102·7
1963—II	2·36	104·0	97·7	101·6	116·5	114·8
1962—IV	2·35	103·7	97·1	100·7	113·7	112·9
1967—IV	2·47	104·5	95·3	99·5	132·4	133·1

Particulars of hours worked are unfortunately available only for industrial employees; we have to assume that the hours worked by the rest of the population have changed similarly. In addition, Table II probably slightly under-estimates the fall in hours worked and the rise in output per man-hour, since in addition to the fall in average weekly hours there has probably been some increase in the average length of the annual holiday.

To obtain estimates of the underlying growth of productivity, we must now adjust output per man-hour for the effects of changes in the number of hours worked (Table III A). From the underlying growth of productivity we obtain the rise in productive potential by allowing both for the remaining effects of the changes in hours worked and for the changes in the number at work (Table III B).

[30]

TABLE III
PRODUCTIVITY AND PRODUCTIVE POTENTIAL
(percentage changes)

A. PRODUCTIVITY

Period	Output per man-hour	40% of change in hours worked	Period	Underlying productivity Average per annum
1952—II to 1959—II	+14·4	+0·7	+15·2	+2·1
1959—II to 1963—II	+11·8	—1·2	+10·5	+2·5
1962—IV to 1967—IV	+17·9	—0·8	+16·9	+3·2

B. PRODUCTIVE POTENTIAL

Period	Underlying productivity	60% of changes in hours worked	Employment	Productive Potential Period	Average per annum
1952—II to 1959—II	+15·2	+1·1	+3·4	+20·4	+2·7
1959—II to 1963—II	+10·5	—1·8	+3·6	+12·5	+3·0
1962—IV to 1967—IV	+16·9	—1·1	+0·8	+16·6	+3·1

It will be seen that, whereas in the two earlier periods the rise in the number at work enabled the increase of productive potential substantially to exceed the increase of productivity, in 1962–67 the slowing-down of the rise in employment, together with the further fall in hours worked, kept the rise of productive potential below that of productivity. It is this, together with the fall of output below productive potential in 1966–67, which until recently has prevented the much accelerated rise in underlying productivity from being reflected in a corresponding acceleration of the rise in output.

It remains to allocate the aggregate rises calculated for each period to particular years within the periods. Since the increases for each of the first two periods approximate extremely closely to those estimated for the same periods by Messrs W. H. Godley and J. R. Shepherd in their paper on 'Long-term Growth and Short-term Policy',[1] we can follow their estimates of annual increases. The closeness of the estimates made here for these two periods to those made by Godley and Shepherd with the use of much more sophisticated statistical methods encourages the hope that our estimates for 1962–67 will provide a valid extrapolation of their series.

[1] National Institute *Economic Review*, August 1964.

Godley and Shepherd estimate that throughout the whole period from 1952 to 1963 the acceleration of the growth of underlying productivity was just under 0·08 per cent a year, raising the rate of increase from 1·85 per cent in 1952–53 to 2·63 per cent in 1962–63. If the same rate of acceleration had continued up to the end of 1967, the rise in productivity from the last quarter of 1962 to the last quarter of 1967 would have been about 15 per cent and the average annual increase for the period under 2·9 per cent, as against the increases of 16·9 per cent and 3·2 per cent shown in Table III. It would seem, therefore, that the acceleration in 1962–67 has been considerably faster than in 1952–63. If we assume a constant rate of acceleration from the second quarter of 1963 onwards, this must have been about 0·25 per cent a year, bringing the annual rise in productivity up from Godley and Shepherd's estimate of 2·63 per cent in 1962–63 to about 3·7 per cent in 1966–67 (Table IV).

TABLE IV

ANNUAL INCREASES IN PRODUCTIVITY AND
PRODUCTIVE POTENTIAL, 1962–67
(percentage changes between 4th quarters)

Years	Productivity	25% of change in standard hours	Employment	Productive potential
1962–63	+2·70	—	+0·4	+3·10
1963–64	+2·95	—0·2	+0·2	+2·95
1964–65	+3·20	—0·6	+0·2	+2·80
1965–66	+3·45	—0·3	—	+3·15
1966–67	+3·70	—	—	+3·70
Total, 1962–67	+16·9	—1·1	+0·8	+16·6
Annual Average	+3·2	—0·2	+0·1	+3·1

To convert the estimated annual increases in productivity into increases in productive potential we have to allow for the effects of changes in hours worked and in the size of the population at work. The number at work rose by 2·8 per cent between the last quarter of 1962 and the last quarter of 1965, and then fell cyclically by 2 per cent, leaving a net increase of 0·8 per cent. Since the rise in the population of working age had levelled off by early 1966, we allocate the whole of the non-cyclical rise of 0·8 per cent to the first three years of the period. Hours worked rose by

1·4 per cent from 1962 to 1963, and then fell by 3·3 per cent from 1963 to 1967, a net fall of 1·9 per cent. Since much of this movement is clearly cyclical, we cannot use the annual changes in hours worked to calculate yearly changes in productive potential. As, however, standard hours (which do not fluctuate cyclically) fell by 4½ per cent during the period, as against a net fall of 1·9 per cent in hours worked, we can deduct 25 per cent of the fall in standard hours instead of 60 per cent of the fall in hours worked. This concentrates the fall in hours on the three middle years of the period. As the result of these adjustments, the steady rise we have assumed for productivity is concealed for productive potential until 1966–67.

In combination with the estimates of Godley and Shepherd for 1952–63, we now have estimates for a continuous series of annual percentage increases of productive potential from 1952 to 1967. We now have only to choose a common base date in order to relate this series to that of output. A convenient date is the last quarter of 1955, when the seasonally adjusted percentage of total unemployment in Great Britain fell to 1 per cent, and the economy can be regarded as having been fully employed—or rather, full employment is defined as a condition similar to that which existed in the last quarter of 1955. By interpolation between the annual figures, we can estimate a quarterly index of productive potential.

The extrapolation of the index beyond the end of 1967 will necessarily be tentative until sufficient evidence has accumulated to enable us to calculate changes between comparable periods. The underlying rate of growth of productivity, which was estimated to have increased from 2·7 per cent in 1962–63 to 3·7 per cent in 1966–67, may well continue to accelerate further. On the other hand, the causes of the acceleration in the past few years may prove to have been temporary, and the rate of growth of productivity may decline again. In either case, however, the rate of growth is unlikely to diverge so rapidly from the 1966–67 growth rate of 3·7 per cent as to make any significant difference in the level of the index of potential for the next year or two, and it seems safest to assume a continuation of a 3·7 per cent rate of growth of productivity until more evidence is available.

It is even more difficult to know how to treat the fall of about 0·3 per cent in the (seasonally adjusted) level of employment in

TABLE V

PRODUCTIVE POTENTIAL, OUTPUT, AND INCOME FROM EMPLOYMENT, 1952 TO 1968

Year and Quarter	Productive Potential 4th Quarter 1955=100	Potential Increase over previous year %	Output 4th Quarter 1955=100	Use of Potential per cent	Income from Employment 4th Quarter 1955=100	Increase over previous year %
1952						
I	90·5		88·1	97·3 ⎫	77·1	+6·9
II	91·1	+2·7	87·1	95·6 ⎬		
III	91·7		88·1	96·1 ⎬	79·7	+7·3
IV	92·3		88·2	95·6 ⎭		
1953						
I	92·9		89·8	96·7 ⎫	82·3	+6·7
II	93·5	+2·6	90·8	97·1 ⎬		
III	94·1		91·8	97·6 ⎬	83·5	+4·8
IV	94·7		93·2	98·4 ⎭		
1954						
I	95·3		93·7	98·3 ⎫	87·1	+5·8
II	95·9	+2·6	94·7	98·6 ⎬		
III	96·5		95·7	99·2 ⎬	89·9	+7·7
IV	97·2		96·8	99·6 ⎭		
1955						
I	97·9		97·1	99·2	93·6 ⎫	+8·6
II	98·6	+2·8	98·0	99·4	95·6 ⎬	
III	99·3		98·8	99·5	98·0 ⎬	+10·1
IV	100·0		100·0	100·0	100·0 ⎭	
1956						
I	100·6		99·2	98·6	102·2	+9·2
II	101·3	+2·7	99·4	98·1	105·1	+9·9
III	102·0		99·2	97·3	106·8	+9·0
IV	102·7		99·7	97·1	108·0	+8·0
1957						
I	103·4		100·8	97·5	109·4	+7·0
II	104·0	+2·7	101·2	97·2	110·3	+4·9
III	104·8		101·7	97·0	112·8	+5·6
IV	105·5		100·7	95·5	113·8	+5·3
1958						
I	106·2		101·3	95·4	115·6	+5·6
II	107·0	+2·9	100·1	93·5	114·8	+4·1
III	107·7		100·8	93·6	115·9	+2·8
IV	108·5		101·9	93·9	117·8	+3·5
1959						
I	109·2		102·2	93·6	118·9	+2·9
II	110·0	+2·8	104·9	95·4	120·5	+4·9
III	110·7		106·3	95·8	122·0	+5·3
IV	111·4		109·1	97·9	124·7	+5·8

the first three-quarters of 1968. We can regard the fall either as cyclical, in which case it does not reduce the rate of growth of productive potential below the rate of growth of productivity, or as non-cyclical, in which case the rate of increase of potential is correspondingly reduced. In Table V and Chart 2, the fall in employment has been treated as non-cyclical, and the estimated increase in productive potential between the last quarter of 1967

Year and Quarter	Productive Potential 4th Quarter 1955=100	Potential Increase over previous year %	Output 4th Quarter 1955=100	Use of Potential per cent	Income from 4th Quarter 1955=100	Employment Increase over previous year %
1960						
I	112·1		110·6	98·7	126·2	+6·1
II	112·8	+2·6	110·8	98·2	129·7	+7·7
III	113·5		111·4	98·1	132·7	+8·8
IV	114·3		112·1	98·1	133·9	+7·5
1961						
I	115·1		113·0	98·2	137·4	+8·9
II	115·9	+2·7	113·4	97·8	141·0	+8·6
III	116·8		113·7	97·3	142·6	+7·4
IV	117·8		112·8	95·8	143·9	+7·5
1962						
I	118·7		113·3	95·4	146·2	+6·4
II	119·7	+3·3	114·6	95·7	148·2	+5·0
III	120·7		115·7	95·9	150·3	+5·4
IV	121·7		115·0	94·5	151·0	+5·0
1963						
I	122·7		(113·7)	(92·7)	(151·7)	(+3·7)
II	123·8	+3·4	117·8	95·2	154·9	+4·5
III	124·6		120·3	96·6	158·1	+5·2
IV	125·5	+3·1	122·2	97·4	161·1	+6·6
1964						
I	126·4		123·4	97·6	164·4	+8·4
II	127·3		125·0	98·2	167·5	+8·2
III	128·2		125·6	98·0	170·9	+8·1
IV	129·2	+2·9	126·8	98·1	174·4	+8·2
1965						
I	130·1		128·3	98·6	176·5	+7·4
II	131·0		127·4	97·3	180·8	+8·0
III	131·9		128·3	97·3	184·8	+8·1
IV	132·8	+2·8	129·5	97·5	188·5	+8·1
1966						
I	133·8		130·3	97·4	192·4	+9·0
II	134·8		130·1	96·5	196·1	+8·5
III	135·9		130·4	96·0	197·9	+7·1
IV	137·0	+3·2	129·6	94·6	195·8	+3·9
1967						
I	138·2		130·3	94·3	196·3	+2·1
II	139·5		131·6	94·3	200·0	+2·0
III	140·7		132·0	93·8	203·1	+2·6
IV	142·0	+3·7	133·7	94·2	207·1	+5·8
1968						
I	143·2		135·6	94·7	211·0	+7·4
II	144·4		135·0	93·5	214·0	+7·0
III	145·6		136·6	93·8	217·2	+7·0
IV	146·8	+3·4	138·1	94·1	220·0	+6·3

and the last quarter of 1968 has therefore been reduced to 3·4 per cent. This figure is rather above that suggested by the Department of Economic Affairs,[1] whose estimate of an average growth of productive potential of just under 3 per cent a year from 1966 to 1972 is obtained by extrapolating the average annual increase of output per head achieved in 1960–66, with an adjustment for

[1] In *The Task Ahead, op. cit.*

CHART 2. PRODUCTIVE POTENTIAL AND OUTPUT

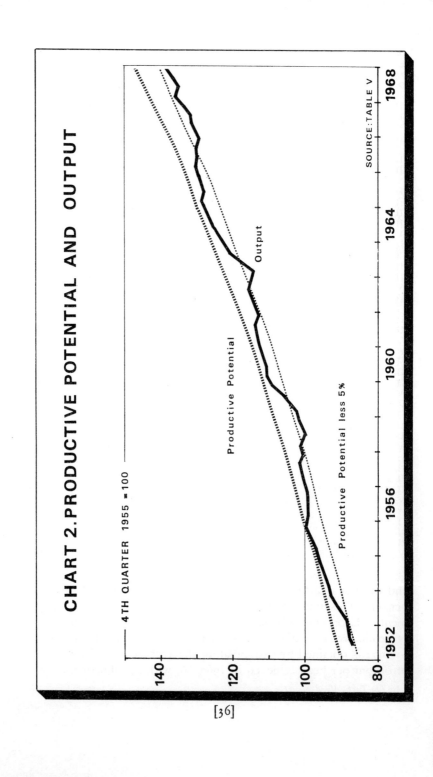

4TH QUARTER 1955 = 100

Productive Potential

Output

Productive Potential less 5%

1952   1956   1960   1964   1968

80   100   120   140

SOURCE: TABLE V

[36]

changes in hours worked, but without any allowance for acceleration either within or after that period. It is, however, well within the margin of error the DEA allow themselves.

In Table V and Chart 2 the quarterly index of productive potential is compared with the quarterly index of gross domestic product, as measured from the output side. The output index is available quarterly in official statistics from the first quarter of 1955. For earlier years, it has been derived from the official annual figures with the help of the index of industrial production. In Chart 2, a line indicating a 95 per cent use of potential has been added as a guide to the eye.

Use of productive potential as indicator

The variations in the percentage of potential in use provide a useful indication of changes in the pressure of demand in the economy. They show clearly the three business cycles between 1952 and 1967. In the first, from 1952 to 1958, the use of potential rises steadily from about 95½ per cent in 1952 to over 99 per cent in 1954 and 100 per cent in the last quarter of 1955. The disinflationary measures at the end of 1955 bring it down sharply in 1956, but it remains at above 97 per cent until a new disinflation in 1957 brings it down to under 94 per cent in 1958.

In the second cycle, from 1958 to 1962, the expansionist budget of 1959 brings a rapid rise in the use of potential, from under 94 in the first quarter of 1959 to over 98 per cent throughout 1960. The 1961 disinflation then brings it down to under 96 per cent in the first three quarters of 1962 and to under 95 per cent in the fourth. Except in the first quarter of 1963 (when an apparent percentage of 92·7 per cent is explained by the exceptional weather), it does not fall as low as in 1958–59.

The third cycle begins with the expansionist budget of 1963, which raises the percentage of potential in use again to over 98 per cent in 1964–65. The third cycle differs from the second in the longer duration of the period of high demand, and it is not until 1966 that the percentage of potential in use falls much below 97½. Since 1966, however, prolonged balance-of-payments difficulties have forced the Government to keep the use of potential continuously below 95 per cent for over two years— longer than in any previous cycle. It can probably be said that the cyclical process is now, at least temporarily, in abeyance.

[37]

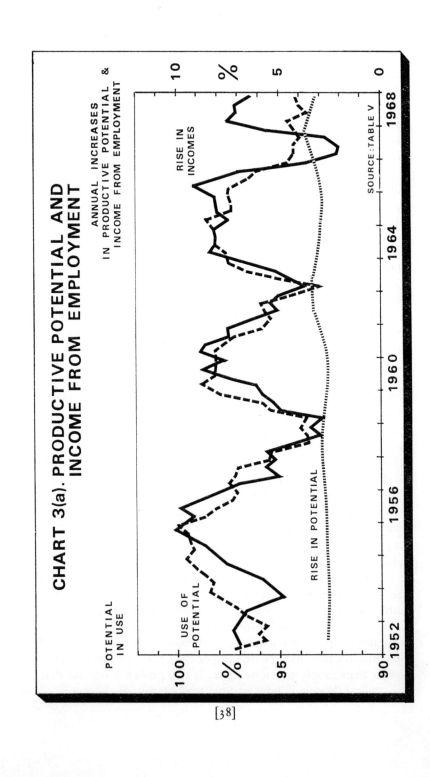

CHART 3(a). PRODUCTIVE POTENTIAL AND INCOME FROM EMPLOYMENT

ANNUAL INCREASES IN PRODUCTIVE POTENTIAL & INCOME FROM EMPLOYMENT

POTENTIAL IN USE

RISE IN INCOMES

USE OF POTENTIAL

RISE IN POTENTIAL

SOURCE: TABLE V

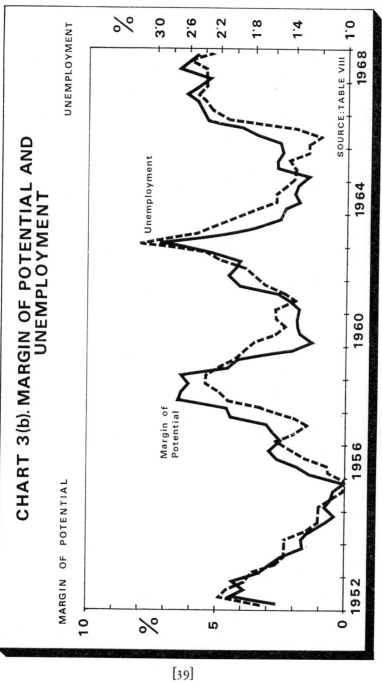

CHART 3(b). MARGIN OF POTENTIAL AND UNEMPLOYMENT

MARGIN OF POTENTIAL

UNEMPLOYMENT

Unemployment

Margin of
Potential

SOURCE: TABLE VIII

If we express the index of output as a percentage of the index of productive potential, the resultant series of the percentage of potential in use provides us with the measure of the pressure of demand in the economy for which we are looking. We now need figures for the rate of rise of incomes with which to compare it. The most appropriate index for this purpose seems to be that of income from employment, easily calculated from the table of factor incomes included in the National Income estimates. This series has the advantage that, like those of productive potential and output, and unlike those of wage-rates and earnings, it includes the effects of changes in the number employed. It is also more comprehensive than the index of weekly earnings, since it includes both the pay of the armed forces and employers' contributions to social security and private pension funds. The official figures are available quarterly from the beginning of 1955, while for earlier years it is possible to break the official annual figures down into half-yearly estimates with the help of the index of weekly earnings.

This index of income from employment, also based on 100 in the last quarter of 1955, is included in Table V, together with a series showing its percentage increase over the corresponding quarter of the previous year. In Chart 3A this last series is compared with that of the percentage of productive potential in use. The two curves are drawn so that a 2 per cent increase in income from employment is equated with a 92 per cent use of potential, and a 10 per cent increase in income with a 100 per cent use of potential. It will be seen that on these scales the two curves move closely together, both in the size and in the timing of the fluctuations. The two main discrepancies are in 1952–54, when the rise in incomes lags more than a year behind the rise in the use of potential, and in 1966–68, when the curve is distorted by the effects of the wage-freeze in the second half of 1966. In spite of these temporary discrepancies, the correlation between the curves is as high as 0·75.

The relationship between the percentage of productive potential in use and the rate of increase of income from employment can also be shown in a different way. In Table VI are shown the results of averaging the percentages of potential in use and the percentage increases in income in periods with given maximum or minimum uses of productive potential. The results range from an annual average income rise of 3·8 per cent for the 13 quarters in which the use of potential was 95 per cent or less to an average rise of 8·4 per cent in the 20 quarters in which the use of potential was over 98 per cent. The average use of potential in all the 66 quarters from the beginning of 1952 to the second quarter of 1968 was 96·7 per cent, and the average rise in employment income 6·6 per cent.

TABLE VI

USE OF PRODUCTIVE POTENTIAL AND
RISE IN INCOME FROM EMPLOYMENT

Number of quarters	Percentage of potential in use		Average annual percentage increase in income from employment
	Range	Average	
13	95 and Under	93·9	3·8
25	96 ,, ,,	94·7	4·9
30	97 ,, ,,	95·0	5·3
46	98 ,, ,,	95·9	5·9
66	All	96·7	6·6
53	Over 95	97·4	7·4
41	,, 96	98·0	7·7
36	,, 97	98·2	7·9
19	,, 98	98·7	8·4

The results shown in Table VI are plotted in Chart 4. It will be seen that all the points lie very close to a straight line curve, from a 2 per cent rise in income with a 92 per cent use of potential to a 10 per cent rise in income with a 100 per cent use of potential. As, however, we do not have data for an average use of potential much below 94 per cent or as high as 99 per cent, we should probably be wise to restrict our conclusions to uses of potential within this range, where we seem to have a reasonably reliable relationship between the percentage of productive potential in use and the rate of increase of income from employment. The reliability of the relationship naturally increases with the length of the period observed; for short periods, it can be considerably disturbed by random variations, especially of output.

It is sometimes asserted, although without much empirical evidence, that the reason for the slower rise of incomes when the

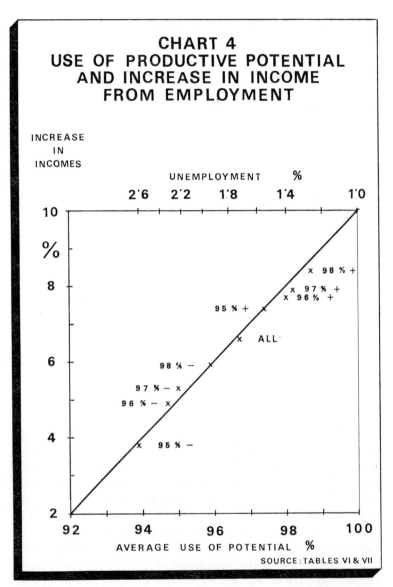

CHART 4
USE OF PRODUCTIVE POTENTIAL
AND INCREASE IN INCOME
FROM EMPLOYMENT

INCREASE
IN
INCOMES

UNEMPLOYMENT %

2·6   2·2   1·8   1·4   1·0

SOURCE: TABLES VI & VII

AVERAGE USE OF POTENTIAL %

margin of unused potential is high is not that the margin is high but that it has recently risen; and it is claimed that, if the margin were maintained at that level for a prolonged period, incomes would begin to rise faster without any fall in the margin. Unfortunately, apart from the period 1967–69, when comparison is invalidated by other factors (see pp 51–60), a high margin of productive potential has never been maintained for long enough to test this contention. The longest period recorded before 1967 was from the second quarter of 1958 to the first quarter of 1959 (when the average margin of unused potential was 6·3 per cent and the annual rate of rise of income 2·9 per cent), which is too short to be conclusive.

It may, however, be possible to test this contention in another way. If it is true that, at any given average margin of unused productive potential, incomes rise more slowly when the margin has risen than when it has fallen, we should expect to find, at similar average margins of potential, that incomes would rise faster on the upswing of the cycle than on the downswing. This we can test from the data given in Table V.

Since 1952 there have been three cyclical upswings, from the fourth quarter of 1952 to the fourth quarter of 1954, from the first quarter of 1959 to the first quarter of 1960 and (if we omit the snowy first quarter of 1963) from the last quarter of 1962 to the second quarter of 1964. There have also been three downswings, from the fourth quarter of 1955 to the second quarter of 1958, from the first quarter of 1961 to the fourth quarter of 1962 and from the first quarter of 1966 to the third quarter of 1967. We cannot, however, use this last downswing, for much of it was affected by the 'wage-freeze' of 1966.

In each cycle the top of the upswing was separated from the beginning of the downswing by a 'plateau', on which the use of potential was maintained at a consistently high level for an appreciable period. The average margins of potential and the average annual increases of income in each of these three stages of the cycle are shown in Table VII.

It will be seen that there is no significant difference between the upswing and the downswing of the cycle in the relationship between the average margin of unused potential and the average rate of income rise, though both periods are strongly differentiated from both the plateaus and the single (usable) example of a 'valley' in 1958–59.

Margin of unused productive potential and unemployment

The only step now needed to complete this section of the discussion is to relate the use of productive potential to the percen-

TABLE VII

MARGINS OF POTENTIAL AND
INCREASES OF INCOMES

Period	Average margin of unused potential	Average annual % increase in income from employment
Up-swings		
1952–4 to 1954–4	2·1	6·3
1959–1 to 1960–1	3·7	5·7
1962–4 to 1964–2	4·0	6·4
Total Up-swings	3·1	6·2
Plateaus		
1954–4 to 1955–4	0·5	9·7
1960–1 to 1961–1	1·7	8·1
1964–2 to 1966–1	2·2	8·3
Total Plateaus	1·6	8·6
Down-swings		
1955–4 to 1958–2	3·0	6·0
1961–1 to 1962–4	3·7	6·2
Total Down-swings	3·3	6·1

tage of unemployment. This task is greatly facilitated by a recent paper by Mr J. R. Shepherd, of the Treasury, entitled 'Productive Potential and the Demand for Labour'.[1] In this he concludes, *inter alia*, that

> 'at the margin, an increase of 1 per cent in output gives rise to a fall of about 1/5 per cent in unemployment when unemployment is already low (300,000), but to a fall of about 1/3 per cent when unemployment is somewhat higher (500,000)'.

If we interpret an increase of 1 per cent in output as the equivalent of a fall of 1 per cent in the margin of unused potential, and assume a ratio of 1 to ¼ at intermediate levels of unemployment, we can construct (Table VIII) a rough scale between various percentage margins of unused potential and the equivalent percentages of unemployment.

---

[1] *Economic Trends*, August 1968.

In Table IX and Chart 3B this scale is used to compare the
margin of unused potential with the percentage of unemployment. It will be seen that, on this scale, the magnitude of the
fluctuations in unemployment corresponds closely to that of
fluctuations in the margin of unused potential. But the Table and
Chart also indicate that changes in unemployment frequently,
though not invariably, lag behind changes in the margin. For
the whole period the lag seems to average about six months, but
its duration varies appreciably from period to period. In 1957,
1960 and 1964 the lag seems to have been considerably more than
six months, while in 1952–53 and in 1961–62 it was almost non-
existent. In the early part of 1966 the lag seems to have been
unusually long, but the gap was closed by the rapid rise of unemployment in the last quarter of that year and since then it
seems to have been very small, although there were some signs
of its re-appearance in 1968.

TABLE VIII

UNEMPLOYMENT AND THE MARGIN OF
UNUSED PRODUCTIVE POTENTIAL

Unemployment Number (thousands)	%	Margin of unused potential %	Unemployment Number (thousands)	%	Margin of unused potential %
233	1·0	0·0	443	1·9	4·0
256	1·1	0·5	466	2·0	4·3
280	1·2	1·0	489	2·1	4·6
303	1·3	1·5	513	2·2	4·9
326	1·4	2·0	536	2·3	5·2
349	1·5	2·4	559	2·4	5·5
373	1·6	2·8	582	2·5	5·8
396	1·7	3·2	606	2·6	6·1
419	1·8	3·6	629	2·7	6·4

If we insert in Chart 4 the scale showing the relationship
between margin of unused potential and the percentage of unemployment given in Table VIII, we can read off the annual
percentage by which (apart from time-lags) income from employment could be expected to increase at any given level of unemployment, ranging from 4 per cent a year with unemployment at about
2·5 per cent to 9 per cent with unemployment at 1·2 per cent.

TABLE IX

MARGIN OF UNUSED POTENTIAL AND UNEMPLOYMENT

Year and Quarter	Margin of unused potential (%)	Unemployment Percentage (Seasonally Corrected) Calculated Current	Calculated Lagged 6 mths.	Actual	Year and Quarter	Margin of unused potential (%)	Unemployment Percentage (Seasonally Corrected) Calculated Current	Calculated Lagged 6 mths.	Actual
1952					**1961**				
I	2·7	1·6	1·3	1·7	I	1·8	1·4	1·4	1·6
II	4·4	2·0	1·4	2·2	II	2·2	1·5	1·4	1·4
III	3·9	1·9	1·6	2·1	III	2·7	1·6	1·4	1·5
IV	4·4	2·0	2·0	1·9	IV	4·2	2·0	1·5	1·7
1953					**1962**				
I	3·3	1·7	1·9	1·8	I	4·6	2·1	1·6	1·8
II	2·9	1·6	2·0	1·6	II	4·3	2·0	2·0	1·9
III	2·4	1·5	1·7	1·5	III	4·1	1·9	2·1	2·2
IV	1·6	1·3	1·6	1·5	IV	5·5	2·4	2·0	2·4
1954					**1963**				
I	1·7	1·3	1·5	1·5	I*	(7·3)	(3·0)	1·9	(3·2)
II	1·4	1·3	1·3	1·3	II	4·8	2·2	2·4	2·5
III	0·8	1·2	1·3	1·2	III	3·4	1·8	(3·0)	2·3
IV	0·4	1·1	1·3	1·2	IV	2·6	1·6	2·2	2·1
1955					**1964**				
I	0·8	1·2	1·2	1·2	I	2·4	1·5	1·8	1·8
II	0·6	1·1	1·1	1·1	II	1·8	1·4	1·6	1·6
III	0·5	1·1	1·2	1·0	III	2·0	1·4	1·5	1·6
IV	0·0	1·0	1·1	1·0	IV	1·9	1·4	1·4	1·5
1956					**1965**				
I	1·4	1·3	1·1	1·1	I	1·4	1·3	1·4	1·4
II	1·9	1·4	1·0	1·1	II	2·7	1·6	1·4	1·4
III	2·7	1·6	1·3	1·3	III	2·7	1·6	1·3	1·5
IV	2·9	1·6	1·4	1·2	IV	2·5	1·5	1·6	1·3
1957					**1966**				
I	2·5	1·6	1·6	1·5	I	2·6	1·5	1·6	1·3
II	2·8	1·6	1·6	1·4	II	3·5	1·8	1·5	1·2
III	3·0	1·7	1·6	1·3	III	4·0	1·9	1·5	1·4
IV	4·5	2·1	1·6	1·4	IV	5·4	2·4	1·8	2·1
1958					**1967**				
I	4·6	2·1	1·7	1·7	I	5·7	2·5	1·9	2·3
II	6·5	2·7	2·1	2·1	II	5·7	2·5	2·4	2·4
III	6·4	2·7	2·1	2·2	III	6·2	2·6	2·5	2·5
IV	6·1	2·6	2·7	2·4	IV	5·8	2·5	2·5	2·4
1959					**1968**				
I	6·4	2·7	2·7	2·4	I	5·3	2·3	2·6	2·4
II	4·6	2·1	2·6	2·2	II	6·5	2·7	2·5	2·4
III	4·2	2·0	2·7	2·0	III	6·0	2·6	2·3	2·6
IV	2·1	1·4	2·1	1·9	IV	5·8	2·5	2·7	2·3
1960									
I	1·3	1·3	2·0	1·8					
II	1·8	1·4	1·4	1·6					
III	1·9	1·4	1·3	1·5					
IV	1·9	1·4	1·4	1·6					

*Note: The figures for the first quarter of 1963 are affected by exceptional weather.

A comparison of Charts 3A and 3B shows that in the only years, 1958 and 1967, in which the rate of rise of income from employment slowed down to equality with the rate of growth of productive potential the percentage of unemployment was about 2½ per cent. So long as the growth of productive potential is maintained at about its present rate, this seems to be the lowest level of unemployment which is, in the long run, compatible with an absence of inflation.

V. EQUILIBRIUM UNEMPLOYMENT IN COMPETITIVE LABOUR CONDITIONS

In the previous Section it was estimated that, in the period from 1952 to 1966, the minimum percentage of unemployment compatible with a rise in income from employment of 4 per cent a year was about 2½ per cent. In this Section an attempt is made to arrive at some idea of the percentage which would be compatible with this objective in a strictly competitive labour market.

We start with the assumption that, in a competitive market, a balance between the demand and supply of labour would result in stable efficiency earnings—that is to say, in a rise of real earnings equal to the rise of productivity, at present estimated at about 3·7 per cent a year. We can obtain some idea of the amounts of labour currently offered and demanded from the official monthly figure of registered unemployment and vacancies, although the unemployment figures cannot be used as they stand. It would seem that the published figures for unemployment considerably exaggerate the number available to fill the vacancies shown as available. There are two main reasons for this discrepancy. The first is that there is a large number of those registered as unemployed who suffer from various personal disabilities which make them 'likely to spend long periods on the registers even when the local demand for labour is high'. The number of such people is put by a survey conducted by the Ministry of Labour in 1964 at about 180,000, or 0·8 per cent of the total number of employees, both employed and unemployed (*Ministry of Labour Gazette*, April 1966).[1] Since many of the disabilities are

[1] On this point, see also J. B. Wood, 'Labour Management and Economic Growth', *Il Politico*, University of Pavia, Vol. XXXII, No. 1, 1967, p. 167.

connected with age, the rise since 1964 in the number of men in the age-group immediately below retirement age may have increased the number suffering from disabilities.

Regional unemployment variations

The other main reason for the difference between the number shown as unemployed and the number effectively able to occupy the situations vacant is the regional distribution of unemployment. Even if the number left after deducting those suffering from disabilities were exactly equal to the number of vacancies, a large surplus of vacancies over unemployment in some regions accompanied by a large surplus of unemployment over vacancies in others would be likely to lead to a faster rise in employment income per person employed than if unemployment and vacancies were in balance in each separate region. This is because an excess supply of labour is less effective in forcing earnings per head down than an excess demand in forcing them up. Instead of forcing earnings per head down until the excess supply of labour is absorbed, the excess supply has the effect merely of causing persistent local unemployment, with the unemployed neither able to obtain work locally at the maintained wage rates nor sufficiently mobile to fill the excess of vacancies in other regions.

The 1964 survey found that the 180,000 unemployed whose disabilities prevented them competing effectively for the work available were distributed very unequally between regions, with the highest percentages in the regions of highest unemployment. In Table X, the non-effectives are deducted from the unemployment totals for each region in October 1968, a month requiring very little seasonal adjustment. The resultant totals of effective unemployment are then compared with the number of vacancies in each region. We find that in the three regions with the highest unemployment percentages, the North of England, Scotland and Wales, there was a surplus of effective unemployment over vacancies of 78,000, or 1·7 per cent of the number of employees. In the regions with moderate unemployment, North-West and South-West England, the Midlands and Yorkshire and Humberside, there was an effective unemployment surplus of 50,000, or 0·5 per cent; and in the low unemployment regions, South-East England (including London) and South and East England, there

TABLE X

UNEMPLOYMENT AND VACANCIES, OCTOBER 1968

Regions	Total Unemployment Thousands	%	Non-effectives Thousands	%	Effective Unemployment Thousands	%	Vacancies Thousands	%	Effective Unemployment less Vacancies Thousands	%
A. High unemployment										
North of England	64	4·84	21	1·59	43	3·25	11	0·83	32	2·42
Scotland	79	3·59	35	1·59	44	2·00	17	0·77	27	1·23
Wales	39	3·90	12	1·20	27	2·70	8	0·80	19	1·90
Total A.	182	4·02	68	1·50	114	2·52	36	0·80	78	1·72
B. Moderate unemployment										
North-West	71	2·40	30	1·01	41	1·39	34	1·15	7	0·24
South-West	34	2·52	10	0·74	24	1·78	15	1·11	9	0·67
Midlands	74	1·99	17	0·46	57	1·53	41	1·10	16	0·43
Yorkshire & Humberside	53	2·60	14	0·69	39	1·91	21	1·03	18	0·88
Total B.	232	2·31	71	0·71	161	1·60	111	1·10	50	0·50
C. Low unemployment										
London and South-East	88	1·55	27	0·48	61	1·07	77	1·36	—16	—0·29
East and South	47	1·68	14	0·50	33	1·18	44	1·57	—11	—0·39
Total C.	135	1·60	41	0·49	94	1·11	121	1·43	—27	—0·32
Total, Great Britain	549	2·36	180	0·78	369	1·58	268	1·15	101	0·43

was a deficiency of effective unemployment of 27,000, or 0·3 per cent. For Great Britain as a whole there was a surplus of effective unemployment of just over 100,000, or slightly more than 0·4 per cent.

We cannot just deduct this surplus from the October 1968 total of unemployment to obtain an estimate of what the total of equilibrium unemployment would be in conditions of competition and equal regional distribution. To do this we must estimate what the totals of unemployment and vacancies would be if they were exactly equated in each region separately. The results of this calculation are shown in Table XI. It will be seen that effective unemployment and vacancies are then equated at a total of 280,000, which, if we add back the non-effectives, gives a total of unemployment of 460,000, or just about 2 per cent.

TABLE XI
EQUILIBRIUM UNEMPLOYMENT, OCTOBER 1968

Regions	Effective Unemployment* Thousands	%	Non-Effective Unemployment Thousands	%	Total Unemployment Thousands	%
A. North of England	12	0·91	21	1·59	33	2·50
Scotland	21	0·95	35	1·59	56	2·54
Wales	12	1·20	12	1·20	24	2·40
Total A.	45	1·00	68	1·50	113	2·50
B. North-West	36	1·21	30	1·01	66	2·22
South-West	17	1·26	10	0·74	27	2·00
Midlands	47	1·27	17	0·46	64	1·73
Yorkshire and Humberside	26	1·27	14	0·69	40	1·96
Total B.	126	1·25	71	0·71	197	1·96
C. London & S. East	69	1·22	27	0·48	96	1·70
East and South	40	1·43	14	0·50	54	1·93
Total C.	109	1·29	41	0·49	150	1·78
Total, Great Britain	280	1·20	180	0·78	460	1·98

*Equals vacancies.

The difference of 120,000, or 0·5 per cent, between this total and the total of 580,000, or 2·5 per cent, which we have estimated to be necessary in present conditions in order to prevent income from employment from rising by more than 4 per cent a year, is due to the combined effects of three factors: the unequal distribution of unemployment; the net monopoly power of labour; and government action to restrain the rise of incomes. In the following paragraph an attempt is made to estimate how much of this effect is due to each of these three causes.

To begin with, it can be said with some confidence that it is not wholly due to regional mal-distribution. In October 1968, with unemployment at 549,000, or substantially below the required level of 580,000, the labour deficiency of 27,000 in the South-East, East and South was probably considerably more than offset by the combined labour surplus of 128,000 in other regions. With total unemployment at 580,000, or 2·5 per cent, a deficiency of under 20,000 in the South-East, East and South would have been much more than outweighed by a surplus of over 140,000 in other regions. If we make a guess and say that a deficiency of labour in the South-East, East and South would just be balanced by a surplus of twice the size in other regions, we arrive at a figure for total unemployment of about 510,000, or 2·2 per cent, leaving 70,000, or 0·3 per cent, as the net effect of labour monopoly and government restraint.

Incomes restraint in 1966–68

We must now turn to the postponed discussion of the anomalous fluctuations in the rate of increase of incomes in 1966–68, revealed in Table V and Chart 3A. The period starts with the dis-inflationary measures of July 1966, which raised the margin of unused productive potential to a level which in previous cycles had been accompanied by a rise of employment incomes of not much more than 4 per cent a year. These measures have been accompanied by vigorous attempts to exercise direct government control over rises in both incomes and prices.

With a margin of unused potential sufficient to equate the supply of labour with the demand, the attempt to restrain rises in wage rates can be seen as an effort to offset the effects of labour monopolies, whether of trade unions or of unofficial groups of key workers. There is therefore no question of the desirability of the objectives of the policy, but merely of its methods and effectiveness. The case for an attempt to exercise direct control over prices is more arguable. Throughout the period, and especially since the devaluation of sterling in November 1967, government policy has been directed, not merely to slowing down the rise of incomes, but also to diverting large amounts of resources, mainly from personal consumption, to exports and to private sector investment. The impact effect of a rise in prices of consumption goods and services is to reduce the volume of consumption. This check to consumption is not offset by a rise in profit margins and business profits, for much of them goes in taxation, some finances increased business investment, and only a small percentage goes to finance increased consumption by shareholders, and that after a long delay. The more successful the control of prices, the larger the increases in taxation needed to prevent consumption from rising.

On a longer view, however, there are two arguments on the other side. One is that the inability to take the easy way of off-setting higher costs by higher prices may force firms to try to offset them by increased efficiency. The other, which is probably more important, is that if employers know that they will, or even may, not be allowed to increase their prices, they may be induced to put up a stronger resistance to demands for wage increases. While these arguments may have some weight for home-based industries serving the home market, they seem to have little relevance to increases of rents, of prices charged for imports, or of prices charged by public authorities and nationalised industries.

Other measures which have accompanied the attempt to control wages and prices have been the heavier taxation of companies, tax discrimination against distributed profits and direct limitation of dividend increases. The purpose of these measures is mainly political; their effect on consumption is minimal.

Until April 1968, the office administering the prices and incomes policy was the Department of Economic Affairs. The responsibility was then transferred to the Ministry of Labour, re-named the Department of Employment and Productivity. Both before and after the transfer, these departments made considerable use of the National Board for Prices and Incomes, first established in April 1965. Up to July 1968, something like a hundred cases had been referred to the Board, almost equally divided between those concerned with prices and those concerned with incomes. The number of cases referred to the Board has increased over time, with almost half the total in the year ending July 1968. Reports have been issued on about three-equarters of the cases referred. Some of the recommendations of the Board have been implemented, especially those dealing with prices. Others have been ignored, or made the basis of a compromise. In a number of their reports, the Board have made recommendations for improving the productivity of the industries concerned. It is possible that these may have contributed to the rise in productivity discussed earlier in this *Paper*, although the acceleration seems to have started some time before the Board was established.

Effectiveness of incomes policy

The extent to which the Board's recommendations have been implemented has depended largely on government policy. Since 1965 this has gone through four phases. Until July 1966, government action was limited to consultation and persuasion; this seems to have been no more effective than similar tactics by earlier governments. In the second half of 1966, however, the government successfully enforced an almost complete standstill on wages and prices, followed by an almost equally successful period of severe restraint in the first half of 1967. Since these measures of restraint were combined with a marked disinflation and a widening of the margin of unused potential, there seemed reason to hope that their effects would be permanent. Unfortunately, the return to voluntary methods in the second half of 1967 showed that the increases had been merely postponed, and in the second half of 1967 and the first quarter of 1968 incomes rose sharply. In March 1968, another strongly disinflationary budget was accompanied by a new period of severe restraint, to last until the end of 1969, with wage increases supposed to be limited to a maximum of $3\frac{1}{2}$ per cent a year, except where a larger increase could be justified by clear evidence of increased productivity.

As is shown in Table XII, the Government succeeded in limiting the rise in income from employment between the second quarter of 1966 and the second quarter of 1967 to no more than 2·0 per cent, as compared with rises of 4·1 per cent and 5·0 per cent respectively in the comparable periods of 1957–58 and 1961–62. In 1967–68, however, the postponed rises in wages brought the increase in employment income up to 7·0 per cent, as against 4·9 per cent in 1958–59 and 4·5 per cent in 1959–60. For the two years together, the 1966–68 rise of 9·2 per cent in employment incomes was exactly the same as in 1957–59, and slightly lower than the rise of 9·7 per cent in 1961–63.

After the second quarter of 1968 no valid comparison with previous cycles is possible, since the second halves of both 1959

TABLE XII

PERSONAL INCOME AND CONSUMPTION

(Second quarters: £ million seasonally adjusted)

	Margin of Unused Potential	At Current Prices				Index of Consumption Prices (1958=100)	At 1958 Prices			
		Income from Employment	Total Personal Income	Disposable Income	Consumption		Income from Employment	Total Personal Income	Disposable Income	Consumption
1957–1959										
1957	2·8	3,201	4,360	3,813	3,608	96·7	3,310	4,509	3,943	3,732
1958	6·5	3,331	4,612	3,975	3,804	100·2	3,324	4,603	3,967	3,797
Avge. 1957–58	4·2									
Inc.		130	252	162	196		14	94	24	65
do. %		4·1	5·8	4·2	5·4	3·6	0·4	2·1	0·6	1·7
1959	4·6	3,495	4,901	4,247	4,021	100·2	3,488	4,891	4,239	4,013
Avge. 1958–59	6·1									
Inc.		164	289	272	217		164	288	272	216
do. %		4·9	6·3	6·8	5·7	—	4·9	6·3	6·9	5·7
Avge. 1957–59	5·1									
Inc.		294	541	434	413		178	382	296	281
do. %		9·2	12·4	11·4	11·4	3·6	5·4	8·5	7·5	7·5
1961–1963										
1961	2·2	4,096	5,722	4,899	4,436	103·8	3,946	5,513	4,720	4,275
1962	4·3	4,300	5,996	5,086	4,730	108·3	3,970	5,536	4,696	4,368
Avge. 1961–62	3·7									
Inc.		204	274	187	294		24	23	—24	93
do. %		5·0	4·8	3·8	6·6	4·3	0·6	0·4	—0·5	2·2
1963	4·8	4,495	6,334	5,360	5,021	109·7	4,098	5,774	4,886	4,579
Avge. 1962–63	5·1									
Inc.		195	338	274	291		128	238	190	211
do. %		4·5	5·6	5·4	6·2	1·3	3·2	4·3	4·0	4·8
Avge. 1961–63	4·5									
Inc.		399	612	461	585		152	261	166	304
do. %		9·7	10·7	9·4	13·2	5·7	3·9	4·7	3·5	7·1

1966–1968

	Margin of Unused Potential	At Current Prices — Income from Employment	Total Personal Income	Disposable Income	Consumption	Index of Consumption Prices (1958=100)	At 1958 Prices — Income from Employment	Total Personal Income	Disposable Income	Consumption
1966	3·5	5,695	7,919	6,576	6,089	121·7	4,675	6,505	5,400	5,003
1967	5·7	5,808	8,257	6,778	6,247	125·3	4,630	6,585	5,400	4,986
Avge. 1966–67	4·9									
Inc.		113	338	202	158		−45	+80	—	−17
do. %		2·0	4·3	3·1	2·6	3·0	−1·0	+1·2	—	−0·3
1968	6·5	6,217	8,909	7,227	6,543	130·7	4,750	6,810	5,540	5,006
Avge. 1967–68	5·9									
Inc.		409	652	449	296		+120	+225	+140	+20
do. %		7·0	7·9	6·6	4·7	4·3	+2·6	+3·4	+2·6	+0·4
Avge. 1966–68	5·4									
Inc.		522	990	651	454		+75	+305	+140	+3
do. %		9·2	12·5	9·9	7·5	7·4	+1·6	+4·7	+2·6	+0·1

and 1963 were periods of rapidly rising output and rapidly falling margins of unused productive potential, while in the second half of 1968 output is estimated to have risen only slightly faster than productive potential.

The rise in income from employment seems to have slowed down appreciably in the second half of 1968, from an increase of 7 per cent between the second quarter of 1967 and the second quarter of 1968 to an annual rate of 5½ per cent (seasonally corrected) between the second and fourth quarters of 1968. Nevertheless, the rise remained a good deal faster than that of about 4 per cent a year which might have been expected, even without an 'incomes policy', on the basis of earlier experience with an average margin of unused productive potential of 6 per cent.

Possible reasons for rapid rise of incomes

(i) Restraints on consumption

On the face of it, these results suggest that the much more vigorous enforcement of an incomes policy in 1966–68 than in either 1957–59 or 1961–63 has on balance had no effect at all. Such an assessment would, however, probably be unjust. Conditions in 1966–68 differed from those of either 1957–59 or 1961–63 in at least two major respects. To begin with, in the earlier periods the Government was concerned only with checking inflation; it was able to obtain the resources needed for improving the balance of payments almost entirely by diverting them from a high rate of stock accumulation. In consequence, it was possible to allow personal consumption to rise quite rapidly in real terms, by an average of 3½ per cent a year or more. In 1966–68, however, the Government was faced with the necessity of diverting to exports very large amounts of resources, not from stock accumulation (which was already inadequate), but mainly from personal consumption. In this it has achieved very considerable success for, after a temporary rise in the last quarter of 1967 and the first quarter of 1968, personal consumption was checked back by the budget to almost exactly the same level in the second quarter as it had stood at in the second quarter of 1966. With the rise in the total (though not the working) population, this must have meant that the average standard of living was appreciably lower than it had been two years before.

[56]

This almost complete check to the rise in consumption was achieved partly by a rapid rise in prices of consumption goods and services and partly (contrary to the general impression) by an increase in personal saving, shown in Table XII as a widening of the difference between disposable income and consumption. The rise in personal saving is in marked contrast with the experience of 1957–59, when there was no increase, and of 1961–63, when there was a fall. It is not surprising that the Government's successful efforts to prevent a rise in the standard of living should have provoked the more vigorous use of whatever monopoly power labour possesses, not only by trade unions but even more by unofficial groups of key workers. Mr Aubrey Jones, chairman of the Prices and Incomes Board, himself believes that the net effect of the Government's incomes policy has been to reduce the rise of prices and incomes by 1 per cent a year below what it would otherwise have been. This claim may be on the optimistic side. But even if we assume that the effect of incomes policy has been to slow down the rise of incomes by only 0·5 per cent a year below what it would otherwise have been, the annual rate of increase of income from employment in the second half of 1968 would without it have been nearly 2 per cent faster than we should have expected on the basis of earlier experience. One possible explanation of this faster rise of incomes is that it is the effect of the increased use by labour of its monopoly power to resist the Government's efforts to hold down the standard of living. If this explanation is correct, the disinflationary measures of November 1968, necessitated by the rapid rise of personal consumption in the second half of the year, and the additional taxation imposed in the 1969 budget, are likely to be followed by maintained pressure for higher wages and a continuation of the over-rapid rise of money incomes.

(ii) *Redundancy payments*

A second recent development which may have helped to induce a faster rise of incomes than was in the past consistent with present levels of unemployment may have been the result of the introduction of redundancy payments and more generous unemployment benefits. These may have reduced the urgency for some of the unemployed to obtain work and may therefore have reduced the pressure of supply on the labour market at any given

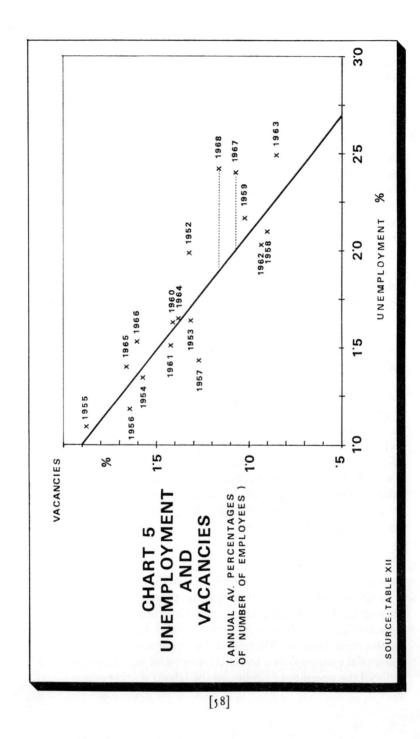

CHART 5
UNEMPLOYMENT
AND
VACANCIES

(ANNUAL AV. PERCENTAGES
OF NUMBER OF EMPLOYEES)

SOURCE: TABLE XII

VACANCIES

%

1·5

1·0

·5

x 1955

1956 x   x 1965

1954 x   x 1966

1961 x   x 1960
          x 1964

1957 x   1953 x

x 1952

x 1968

x 1967

x 1959

1962 x
1958 x

x 1963

1·0   1·5   2·0   2·5   3·0

UNEMPLOYMENT   %

level of unemployment. Some confirmation of this view is provided by the fact that in both 1967 and 1968 the number of employment vacancies was considerably larger than has in the past accompanied similar levels of unemployment. In Table XIII and Chart 5 an attempt is made to measure the present divergence from earlier experience.

TABLE XIII

UNEMPLOYMENT AND VACANCIES IN
GREAT BRITAIN, 1952 to 1968

(Annual average percentages of number of employees)

Year	Unemployment	Vacancies	Year	Unemployment	Vacancies
1952	1·99	1·32	1961	1·51	1·42
1953	1·64	1·31	1962	2·03	0·93
1954	1·34	1·57	1963	2·49	0·85
1955	1·09	1·88	1964	1·65	1·38
1956	1·18	1·64	1965	1·40	1·66
1957	1·43	1·27	1966	1·53	1·60
1958	2·10	0·90	1967	2·40	1·07
1959	2·17	1·02	1968	2·42	1·16
1960	1·63	1·41			

The number of unemployed tends normally to move inversely with the number of vacancies; the only development which tends to make them move in the same direction is a rise in the whole scale of the system as a result of an increase in the size of the working population. We can get rid of this distortion by expressing in Table XIII both unemployment and vacancies as percentages of the number of employees. It will be seen from Chart 5 that, on the average of earlier experience, we should have expected the 1·1 per cent of vacancies recorded in 1967 to be accompanied by an average level of unemployment of about 2·0 per cent, and the 1·2 per cent of vacancies in 1968 by about 1·9 per cent of unemployment, as against actual average unemployment of about 2·4 per cent in both years.

(iii) *Increase in structural unemployment*

An alternative, or additional, explanation, put forward both by the DEA[1] and by the National Institute[2] to account for the divergence in 1967–68 from previous experience in the relationship between unemployment and vacancies, is that an increased proportion of the unemployment recorded is structural rather

[1] *The Task Ahead, op. cit.*, p. 42.
[2] National Institute *Economic Review*, February 1969, p. 28.

than cyclical, and is due to the fact that an increased proportion of the unemployed is not of the type needed to fill the available vacancies—in particular, that the unsatisfied demand is for skills which few of the unemployed are able to supply.

It seems possible that both types of explanation may help to account for the over-rapid rise of incomes in 1967–68. The explanation that it has been due to labour's resistance to the Government's efforts to restrain consumption obtains some support from the fact that the slowing-down of the rise of incomes in the second half of 1968 was accompanied by quite a substantial recovery in personal consumption. It also helps to account for the increase in the frequency of strikes, especially unofficial strikes, which has recently induced the Government to put forward measures designed to discourage them. If it is correct, the effectiveness of the Government's measures to discourage strikes may be small so long as it is obliged to continue to hold down personal consumption.

While the checking of the rise of personal consumption may account for the increased pressure for higher money incomes and for the increased frequency of strikes, it does not explain the change which seems to have taken place in the relationship between unemployment and vacancies, as do the second and third explanations. One test of the relative importance of the different explanations will be to see what happens when, at last, consumption can again be allowed to rise proportionately with national income. In so far as the first explanation is valid, the relationship between the level of unemployment and the rate of rise of incomes can then be expected to return towards that shown in Chart 4. If, on the other hand, either the second or the third explanation is correct, the level of unemployment corresponding to any given rise of incomes will be found to have permanently increased to above that found in the period 1952–66.

VI. EXCESS DEMAND AND THE BALANCE OF PAYMENTS

The effects on the balance of payments of an over-rapid rise of output and a consequent shrinking of the margin of unused productive potential seem to take three forms. The first appears as a direct result of the faster rise of output, which increases the demand for imported materials. This effect is accentuated by a rise in the rate of stock accumulation. The rises, both in imports and in stocks, usually appear only after a time-lag of about nine months, and therefore affect the annual totals only in the second year of the upturn. Since this worsening of the balance of payments usually brings with it the first tentative steps to restrain demand, and since these are shortly followed by a slowing-down of the rise of output, the check to output is usually attributed to the effects of the worsening balance of payments. However, by the second year of each upturn (1954, 1960, 1964) the margin of unused potential had already fallen so low that the rate of growth of output had in any case to fall towards that of potential. The most, therefore, that a restriction of demand could do at this stage was to anticipate by a very few months the inevitable slowing-down of the rise of output.

In the 1958–61 and the 1962–66 cycles, as will be seen from Table XIV, the main rise in the rate of stock accumulation and the main worsening of the balance of payments appeared in the second years of the upturn, 1960 and 1964. In the 1952–57 cycle, exceptionally, these developments did not appear until 1955, the third year of upturn. There was a special reason for this postponement. In 1954 the Government sold off large quantities of reserve stocks accumulated during the Korean War, so that the sharp rise in private sector stocks was more than offset by the fall in Government stocks, and total stock accumulation fell. The smaller further fall in government stocks in 1955 again kept total stock accumulation below that of the private sector, and probably prevented the adverse balance of payments from being larger than it was.

The inverse cyclical relationship between the balance of payments and the rate of stock accumulation, which is clearly shown in Table XIV, implies that a favourable balance of payments which is accompanied by an abnormally small rise in stocks is likely to be a precarious one; while, given adequate foreign exchange reserves, an adverse balance which is accompanied by an exceptionally large rise in stocks should not, by itself, give rise to undue anxiety. Even apart from the need to repay the foreign short-term debts incurred in recent years, the UK needs a current account surplus of something like £300 million a year, or rather over 0·8 per cent of the present gross national product, to permit the removal of restrictions on long-term foreign investment.

[61]

TABLE XIV

BALANCE OF PAYMENTS AND STOCK ACCUMULATION

Years	Increase in output over previous year (%)	Average margin of unused productive potential (%)	Balance of payments on Current a/c £m	% of GNP	Stock Accumulation Public Sector £m	Private Sector £m	Total £m	% of GNP	Balance of Payments plus Stocks £m	% of GNP
1952	−0·7	3·8	+163	+1·2	+128	−78	+50	+0·4	+213	+1·5
1953	+4·0	2·5	+145	+1·0	+27	+98	+125	+0·8	+270	+1·8
1954	+4·2	1·1	+117	+0·7	−188	+244	+56	+0·4	+173	+1·1
1955	+3·4	0·5	−155	−0·9	−93	+393	+300	+1·8	+145	+0·9
1956	+0·9	2·2	+208	+1·1	−8	+267	+259	+1·4	+467	+2·5
1957	+1·7	3·2	+233	+1·2	+18	+220	+238	+1·2	+471	+2·4
Average 1952-57	+2·3	2·2	+118	+0·7	−19	+191	+172	+1·0	+290	+1·7
1958	−0·1	5·9	+344	+1·7	+28	+83	+111	+0·5	+455	+2·2
1959	+4·5	4·3	+143	+0·7	+1	+173	+174	+0·8	+317	+1·5
1960	+5·4	1·7	−265	−1·2	−42	+637	+595	+2·6	+330	+1·4
1961	+1·8	2·7	−4	—	+4	+319	+323	+1·3	+319	+1·3
Average 1958-61	+2·9	3·6	+55	+0·3	−2	+303	+301	+1·3	+356	+1·6
1962	+1·3	4·6	+112	+0·4	+11	+58	+69	+0·3	+181	+0·7
1963	+3·3	4·5	+111	+0·4			+228	+0·8	+339	+1·2
1964	+6·0	2·0	−399	−1·4			+677	+2·3	+278	+0·9
1965	+2·4	2·3	−91	−0·3			+436	+1·4	+345	+1·1
1966	+1·3	3·9	+5	—			+259	+0·8	+264	+0·8
Average 1962-66	+2·9	3·5	−52	−0·2			+334	+1·1	+282	+0·9
1967	+1·4	5·9	−399	−1·2			+184	+0·5	−215	−0·6
1968	+3·4	5·9	−419	−1·2			+236	+0·7	−183	−0·5

With an average rate of stock accumulation equal to about 1·2 per cent of GNP, the aggregate of balance of payments plus stock accumulation needed for long-term viability is thus rather over 2 per cent of GNP. With the additional need to repay short-term foreign debts, the Government has set its sights higher than this, at a balance-of-payments surplus of £500 million or about 1·4 per cent of GNP. This implies a total of balance of payments plus stock accumulation equal to about 2·6 per cent of GNP—a level which has been approached since the war only in the period 1956–58. Provided that the combined total can be raised to, and maintained at, this level, temporary changes in the relative proportions of the two items can be disregarded.

If this first effect on the balance of payments were the only result of an over-rapid rise of output, it would be possible for a country with adequate reserves of foreign exchange to disregard it. Unfortunately there are two others. Even after the rate of rise of output has fallen to equality with that of productive potential, the maintenance of an inadequate margin of unused potential is likely to be accompanied by long order books, delays in delivery, and the development of bottle-necks. It therefore tends both to lose exports and to cause local users to obtain urgently needed goods from abroad. Statistical evidence of this effect is difficult to obtain, since, in the short run, developments abroad may be as important as those at home. Some evidence is perhaps provided by Table XIV, with the progressive fall of balance of payments plus stocks, as a percentage of GNP, from 1953 to 1955 and from 1959 to 1961. A similar fall in 1964–66 seems to have been temporarily interrupted in 1965 by the imposition of the import surcharge.

Inflation, export costs and the balance of payments

Most serious of all the effects of a period of excess demand is a permanent rise in the level of costs and prices. If the rise in costs is faster than that in other industrial countries, the competitive power of domestic producers will be permanently impaired, both in home and export markets. As Table XV shows, the rapid rise in British labour costs per unit of output has caused both British costs to rise faster than export prices, thus making exports less profitable, and prices of British manufactured exports to rise faster than those of most other countries, thus making British exports less competitive.

[63]

TABLE XV

UK LABOUR COSTS AND DOLLAR EXPORT PRICES
OF MANUFACTURES

(1958 = 100)

	UK Labour Costs			Dollar Export Prices of Manufactured Goods					
	Output	Income from Employment	Labour Cost Per unit of Output	UK	USA	Germany	France	Italy	Japan
1952	87·0	67·6	77·7	94	89	106	104	119	115
1953	90·5	71·5	79·0	91	89	100	98	115	108
1954	94·3	76·3	80·9	90	88	96	97	111	103
1955	97·5	83·4	85·5	92	90	96	97	106	98
1956	98·4	91·0	92·5	94	94	99	102	100	101
1957	100·1	96·1	96·0	99	99	100	102	104	105
1958	100·0	100·0	100·0	100	100	100	100	100	100
1959	104·5	104·7	100·2	100	103	100	94	93	100
1960	110·1	112·6	102·3	102	105	102	97	96	102
1961	112·1	121·6	108·5	103	106	107	97	93	98
1962	113·6	128·4	113·0	105	106	108	97	88	95
1963	117·4	134·7	114·7	107	106	107	98	94	93
1964	124·4	146·0	117·5	109	106	108	101	96	92
1965	127·7	157·4	123·2	112	110	110	103	94	92
1966	129·4	168·4	130·1	117	113	112	106	93	90
1967	131·2	173·7	132·1	116	116	111	106	93	92
1968	135·7	185·8	136·9	108*	118	111	105	89	92

*Sterling Price Index = 126.

It is this rise in British costs which has probably been the main reason for the deterioration of the balance of payments, especially since 1962. It is true that, as Table XVI shows, the progressive rise of government expenditure abroad has been an important contributory factor; but of the deterioration of £108 million in the average balance on current account between the 1958–61 and the 1962–66 cycles, £65 million was due to the worsening of the visible balance, and only £43 million to the faster rise in government expenditure abroad than in the net invisible earnings of the private sector. It is likely that the visible balance would also have fallen sharply between the 1952–57 and the 1958–61 cycles if it had not been for the substantial improvement in the terms of visible trade, due mainly to the sharp fall in 1957–58 in prices of imported foodstuffs and raw materials, which much more than offset the deterioration in the terms of trade for services. Between the 1958–61 and the 1962–66 cycles, on the other hand, a moderate further improvement in the terms of visible trade was entirely offset by the further deterioration in the terms of trade for services.

TABLE XVI

TERMS OF TRADE AND BALANCE OF PAYMENTS

Terms of Trade (1958 = 100)

	Average 1952–57	Average 1958–61	Average 1962–66	1967	1968 Jan.–June	July–Dec.
GOODS						
Export Prices	95	100	107	115	123	126
Import Prices	106	99	102	106	118	120
Terms of Trade	90	101	105	108	104	105
SERVICES						
Export Prices	98	102	104	108	114	115
Import Prices	93	107	117	130	145	145
Terms of Trade	105	95	89	83	79	79
GOODS AND SERVICES						
Export Prices	96	101	106	113	121	123
Import Prices	103	101	106	112	123	126
Terms of Trade	93	100	100	101	98	98

Balance of Payments on Current Account (£ million)

					Jan.–June	July–Dec.
COMMODITY TRADE						
Exports and Re-exports	3033	3638	4525	5026	2927	3176
Imports	3202	3799	4751	5661	3387	3512
Visible Balance	—169	—161	—226	—635	—460	—336
NET INVISIBLES						
Government	—119	—265	—418	—466	—237	—225
Other	+407	+481	+591	+702	+428	+411
Invisible Balance	+288	+216	+173	+236	+191	+186
Balance of Payments	+119	+55	—53	—399	—269	—150

As Table XV shows, the devaluation of sterling in November 1967 seems to have about restored the competitive position of British exports, and, which is perhaps at least as important, to have appreciably improved the profitability of exporting. It is essential that these improvements should be maintained, especially until the enormous foreign short-term debts contracted in recent years have been repaid. This repayment seems likely to take many years to achieve. The Treasury's economic forecasts, which accompanied the 1969 budget, indicated that the balance of trade in goods and services, at 1958 prices, seasonally corrected, was expected to improve from an import surplus of £140 million in the second half of 1968 to an export surplus of only £30 million in the first half of 1970, in spite of the fact that consumption expenditure was expected to rise by little more than one-half of one per cent over this period.

In the absence of an improvement, of which there has hitherto
been little sign, in the terms of trade for goods and services
combined, of a substantial further increase in net investment
income from abroad or a substantial decrease in transfer payments
(mainly on government account) to abroad, an estimated balance-
of-trade surplus in goods and services at 1958 prices of £30
million implies a current account surplus at current prices of
barely £50 million in the first half of 1970. This would be an
improvement of barely £200 million in 18 months over the
current account deficit of £150 million in the second half of 1968.
A current account surplus at the rate of barely £100 million a year
would be only just enough to cover normal net exports of long-
term capital even under present restrictions, and would leave
nothing for the net repayment of foreign short-term debt. A
continuation of the improvement in the half-yearly current
account balance at the rate of £200 million every 18 months
would mean that the target of a £500 million surplus would be
reached about the second half of 1971. On these assumptions
which, on the trading results for the first four months of 1969,
look over-optimistic, net repayments of short-term debt could
probably begin on a small scale in the second half of 1970, but
the repayment of the whole debt of something like £3,000 million
would not be completed until towards the end of the 1970s.

It is true that, appreciably before then, increasing confidence in
sterling might have removed our foreign creditors' desire for
repayment. But, even so, it would be necessary, in order to
permit the removal of restrictions on exports of long-term capital
and to maintain confidence in sterling, to maintain a current
account surplus of £300 million a year or more. This means that
the country must never again allow incomes to rise as much
faster than output as they have done in recent years. And this
again implies, as does the Treasury projection for the period up
to 1970, that the country must from now on be prepared to maintain a larger average margin of unused productive potential, and
a higher average level of unemployment, than those to which
the post-war generation has become accustomed.

Note: (June 1971)

The foregoing assessment of the balance-of-payments position, as it appeared in April 1969, proved to be much too pessimistic. A few months later it was discovered that exports had been increasingly under-recorded for several years, and the estimated deficit on current account for 1968 has therefore been reduced from £419 million to £306 million. For the same reason, the seasonally corrected surplus for the first half of 1969 is now put at £109 million, as compared with the £50 million estimated above. For the whole year 1969 the current surplus was £437 million, and for 1970, with the help of a marked improvement in the terms of trade in the second half of the year, £631 million.

Cost-push at last

I. RAPID RISE OF INCOMES
'UNFORESEEN DEVELOPMENT'

At the end of the third quarter of 1969 it seemed as if Great Britain was at last emerging from many years of economic difficulty. With the help both of the competitive advantage provided by the devaluation of 1967 and of the diversion to exports of resources from home use, the balance of payments on current account had achieved a surplus large enough to permit the commencement of substantial repayments of the emergency loans, totalling over £3,000 million, obtained from the International Monetary Fund and foreign central banks during the previous five years. The improvement in the balance of trade can be seen in Table XVII, which shows that between 1967 and 1969 it absorbed 2·3 per cent of gross domestic product (nearly half the growth of total output) at the expense of personal consumption and public expenditure.

Once the required export surplus had been achieved, and needed only to be maintained, it was possible to look forward to a resumed rise in the domestic use of resources, and especially in real personal consumption, at a rate in line with the growth of productive potential, estimated at about 3 per cent a year (equivalent to a rise of about $3\frac{1}{2}$ per cent a year in output per man-hour).

Unfortunately, in the last quarter of 1969, signs of a new and unforeseen development appeared. In spite of a slight widening of the margin of unused productive potential and of a small rise in unemployment, the annual rate of rise in income from employment[1] accelerated, as Table XVIII shows, from 6·9 per cent between the first three quarters of 1968 and the first three quarters of 1969 to 8·3 per cent in the last quarter of 1969, 10·4 per cent in the first half of 1970 and 13·7 per cent in the second half. The 1970 rise in employment incomes has been enormously faster than could have been expected from the experience of 1952–66, summarised in Table XIX. Already in the first three quarters of 1969 the rise of 6·9 per cent had been considerably faster than the 4·8 per cent which could have been expected, on the basis of

---

[1] Comprising wages, salaries, forces' pay, and employers' national insurance and pensions contributions.

TABLE XVII

CHANGES IN USE OF GROSS DOMESTIC PRODUCT, 1967 AND 1969
(At 1963 market prices)

	£ million				Percentages of GDP at 1963 market prices		
	1967	1969	Change	Change (%)	1967	1969	Change
Personal Consumption	22,075	22,681	+606	+2·7	64·8	63·4	−1·4
Public Auth. Ct. Exp. on Goods & Services	5,855	5,814	−41	−0·7	17·2	16·2	−1·0
Gross Domestic Fixed Capital Formation:							
Public Sector	3,159	2,971	−188	−6·0	9·3	8·3	−1·0
Private Sector	3,346	3,711	+365	+10·9	9·8	10·4	+0·6
Total	6,505	6,682	+177	+2·7	19·1	18·7	−0·4
Increase in Stocks	184	357	+173		0·5	1·0	+0·5
Exports of Goods and Services	6,572	8,052	+1,480	+22·5	19·3	22·5	+3·2
Imports of Goods and Services	7,120	7,792	+672	+9·4	20·9	21·8	+0·9
Balance of Trade do.	−548	+260	+808		−1·6	+0·7	+2·3
GDP at Market Prices	34,071	35,794	+1,723	+5·1	100·0	100·0	100·0

Table XIX, with a 5·2 per cent margin of unused productive potential. With the wider margin of 6·4 per cent of potential in 1970, the annual rise in income from employment to be expected on the basis of pre-1966 experience was less than 4 per cent, as against the rise of nearly 14 per cent recorded between the second half of 1969 and the second half of 1970. The discrepancy between the expected and the actual rates of rise in employment incomes therefore widened from 2·1 per cent in the first three quarters of 1969 to about 10 per cent in the second half of 1970.

If, instead of the margin of unused productive potential, we use the percentage of unemployment as a basis for comparison, we get approximately the same result. With an unemployment percentage of 2·4, we should have expected a rise of employment incomes in the first three quarters of 1969 of 4·5 per cent, as compared with the actual rise of 6·9 per cent. With unemployment at over 2·6 per cent in the second half of 1970, we should have expected, from Table XIX, an income rise of 3·8 per cent, as against an actual rise of 13·7 per cent, again a discrepancy of about 10 per cent.

This enormous discrepancy seems to have been due to two separate and independent causes. A clue to the first, and less important, of these is given by the figures of unfilled employment vacancies. As Table XIX shows, up to 1966 vacancies vary inversely with unemployment, with 2·4 per cent of unemployment accompanied by about 0·75 per cent of vacancies and 2·6 per cent of unemployment by about 0·6 per cent of vacancies. But in 1969, as Table XVIII shows, the percentage of vacancies was not 0·75 but 1·23, and in 1970 not 0·6 but 1·12. Table XIX indicates that before 1966 1·23 per cent of vacancies could have been expected to be accompanied by a rise of about 6·4 per cent in income from employment, and 1·12 per cent of vacancies by a rise of nearly 6 per cent. If, therefore, we use unfilled vacancies as a basis of comparison, instead of either the margin of unused potential or unemployment, we can account for most of the discrepancy in the first three quarters of 1969 and for over 2 per cent of the 10 per cent discrepancy in the second half of 1970.

Of the various explanations advanced to account for the change since 1966 in the relationship between unemployment and unfilled vacancies, the likeliest, on grounds both of logic and of timing, seems to be the introduction of redundancy payments and higher

USE OF PRODUCTIVE POTENTIAL, UNEMPLOYMENT AND UNFILLED VACANCIES
ANNUAL PERCENTAGE INCREASES IN HOURLY WAGE RATES, WEEKLY EARNINGS AND INCOME FROM EMPLOYMENT, 1963–70

Year	Index of Productive Potential	Index of Output (4th Quarter 1955=100 Seasonally Adjusted)	Use of Productive Potential (4th Quarter 1955=100 Seasonally Adjusted)	Margin of Unused Potential	Unemployment Seasonally Adjusted (Percentage of Employees Employed and Unemployed in GB)	Unfilled Vacancies Seasonally Adjusted (Percentage of Employees Employed and Unemployed in GB)	Hourly Wage Rates (Percentage Increase over Corresponding Period of Previous Year)	Weekly Earnings Seasonally Adjusted	Income from Employment Seasonally Adjusted
1963	124·2	118·7	95·6	4·4	2·49	0·85	3·7		5·1
1964	127·8	125·6	98·3	1·7	1·65	1·38	5·2	7·2	8·3
1965	131·6	128·9	97·9	2·1	1·40	1·66	6·3	7·4	8·0
1966	135·5	131·1	96·8	3·2	1·53	1·60	6·7	6·5	7·0
1967	140·5	133·3	94·7	5·3	2·40	1·07	4·0	3·3	4·1
1968	145·2	138·3	95·2	4·8	2·43	1·16	6·9	8·1	6·8
1969	149·6	141·7	94·7	5·3	2·42	1·23	5·3	7·8	7·3
1970	154·1	144·3	93·6	6·4	2·62	1·12	10·2	12·0	12·1
Year and quarter									
1969 I	148·0	140·2	94·7	5·3	2·41	1·23	5·3	7·3	6·3
II	149·1	141·7	95·0	5·0	2·37	1·24	5·2	7·8	7·3
III	150·2	142·1	94·6	5·4	2·43	1·23	5·1	7·9	7·0
IV	151·3	142·7	94·3	5·7	2·45	1·21	5·6	8·3	8·3
1970 I	152·4	143·1	93·9	6·1	2·56	1·17	7·4	10·1	9·3
II	153·5	143·8	93·7	6·3	2·62	1·11	9·4	11·2	11·6
III	154·6	144·8	93·5	6·5	2·67	1·13	10·6	13·0	13·8
IV	155·8	145·6	93·5	6·5	2·60	1·07	13·0	13·8	13·6
1971 I	157·0	144·4	92·0	8·0	2·97	0·87	13·4	12·7	11·8
II	158·1				3·41	0·76	12·7		
Treasury Projection									
1971 1st Half	157·5	144·3	91·6	8·4					
2nd Half	159·9	146·7	91·7	8·3					
1972 1st Half	162·3	148·8	91·7	8·3					

unemployment benefits in 1965 and 1966. These have apparently enabled many of those becoming unemployed to wait longer in the hope of obtaining work of a preferred type instead of having to accept the first available vacancy. There has therefore tended to be a reduction, at any given level of unemployment, in the supply of labour coming forward to fill the available vacancies.

TABLE XIX

AVERAGE RELATIONSHIPS IN 1952–66 BETWEEN MARGIN OF UNUSED POTENTIAL, UNEMPLOYMENT, VACANCIES AND INCOME FROM EMPLOYMENT

Margin of Unused Productive Potential (%)	Unemployment	Unfilled Vacancies	Annual Increase in Employment Incomes (%)
	Percentage of Employees		
0·0	1·0	1·90	10·0
0·5	1·1	1·82	9·5
1·0	1·2	1·74	9·0
1·5	1·3	1·65	8·5
2·0	1·4	1·57	8·0
2·4	1·5	1·49	7·6
2·8	1·6	1·41	7·2
3·2	1·7	1·32	6·8
3·6	1·8	1·24	6·4
4·0	1·9	1·16	6·0
4·3	2·0	1·08	5·7
4·6	2·1	0·99	5·4
4·9	2·2	0·91	5·1
5·2	2·3	0·83	4·8
5·5	2·4	0·75	4·5
5·8	2·5	0·66	4·2
6·1	2·6	0·58	3·9
6·4	2·7	0·50	3·6
6·7	2·8	0·41	3·3
7·0	2·9	0·32	3·0

Sources: Table VI (p. 41), Chart 4 (p. 42) and Chart 5 (p. 58), of this Hobart Paper.

A comparison of Table XVIII with Table XIX indicates that the result has been an increase in the rate of rise of employment incomes at any given level of unemployment by over 2 per cent above the pre-1966 rate of increase. Conversely, it indicates that the percentage of unemployment needed, in a free labour market, to achieve a given rise of employment incomes is about 0·6 per cent higher than before 1966. Thus the percentage of unemployment consistent with an income rise of 4 per cent a year has risen from about 2·6 per cent to about 3·2 per cent. It is unfortunate that measures taken to make a somewhat higher level of un-employment politically and socially acceptable should have in-creased the amount of unemployment needed, in a free labour market, to prevent an over-rapid rise of employment incomes.

If the foregoing argument is accepted, nearly all the rise of employment incomes up to the third quarter of 1969 can be attributed to the employers' demand for labour and very little to the use of monopoly power by labour. There are two possible explanations for this: (i) that labour made little attempt to exert monopoly power; and (ii) that the attempt was made, but was frustrated by the government's incomes policy, the collapse of which in the summer of 1969 opened the flood-gates. The truth probably lies more with the first explanation than with the second. The effect of the incomes policy, though perhaps perceptible, was probably small. The Prices and Incomes Board itself put it at a slowing-down of the rate of income increase by about 1 per cent a year, and even this may have been an over-estimate. Even, however, if the direct effect of incomes policy had been small, its spectacular collapse in the summer of 1969 may have had a con-siderable psychological effect, and may have helped to trigger off the subsequent wave of extravagant wage demands.

While the 1965–66 increases in unemployment benefits seem to have accounted for most of the difference between the expected and actual rises in employment incomes up to the third quarter of 1969, they account for not much more than 2 per cent out of the 10 per cent discrepancy in the second half of 1970. The remainder, amounting to nearly 8 per cent, must be ascribed wholly to 'cost-push'—the use of monopoly power by trade unions and shop-stewards. The country has thus reached the position, envisaged on page 51, where

'the attempt to restrain rises in wage rates can be seen as an effort to offset the effects of labour monopolies, whether of trade unions or of unofficial groups of key workers. There is therefore no question of the desirability of the objectives of the policy, but merely of its methods and effectiveness'.

It is unfortunate that the ineffective use of 'incomes policy' to hold down rises in employment incomes caused by the demand for labour should have discredited it just at the moment when its use, for the first time, may have become appropriate.

II. REPERCUSSIONS OF BALANCE-OF-PAYMENTS POLICY

While the breakdown of the Labour government's incomes policy may have contributed to the rapid acceleration of the rise of employment incomes, the main cause is almost certainly to be found in the success of its efforts to improve the balance of payments. For this purpose it was necessary to restrict the domestic use of resources, during 1966–67 in order to reduce the pressure of aggregate demand and in 1968–69 to divert resources to exports. This was achieved (i) by severe restraints on public expenditure; (ii) by a restrictive monetary policy, which tended to slow down the rise of private sector investment; (iii) as Table XX shows, by raising market prices of consumption goods and services in 1968 and 1969 much above their factor cost prices, in 1968 partly through the higher import prices resulting from

TABLE XX

PERCENTAGE INCREASES IN PRICES OVER CORRESPONDING PERIOD OF PREVIOUS YEAR, 1963–70

Year	Factor Cost Prices of GDP	Effect of Indirect Taxes and Subsidies	Market Prices of GDP	Effect of Import Prices	Market Prices of Final Product	Prices of Consumer Goods and Services	Retail Prices
1963	2·1	—0·1	2·0	+0·1	2·1	1·9	2·0
1964	2·6	+0·3	2·9	+0·1	3·0	3·2	3·3
1965	4·1	+1·0	5·1	—0·7	4·4	4·6	4·8
1966	3·5	+0·9	4·4	—0·5	3·9	3·8	3·9
1967	3·7	—0·5	3·2	—0·5	2·7	2·5	2·5
1968	2·7	+1·1	3·8	+1·2	5·0	4·5	4·7
1969	3·5	+1·6	5·1	—0·5	4·6	5·3	5·4
1970	7·9	—0·7	7·2	—0·4	6·8	5·5	6·4
Av. 1963–70	3·8	+0·4	4·2	—0·1	4·1	3·9	4·1
Year and quarter							
1969 I	3·1	+2·4	5·5	—0·4	5·1	6·0	6·2
II	3·4	+1·5	4·9	—0·6	4·3	5·0	5·4
III	2·6	+2·2	4·8	—0·4	4·4	5·0	5·0
IV	4·5	+0·6	5·1	—0·3	4·8	5·1	5·1
1970 I	5·3	+0·2	5·5	—0·4	5·1	4·6	5·0
II	7·0	—0·2	6·8	—0·3	6·5	5·0	5·8
III	9·6	—1·4	8·2	—0·7	7·5	5·9	6·9
IV	9·4	—0·8	8·6	—0·8	7·8	6·1	7·7
1971 I	10·5						8·6

[74]

devaluation and partly through higher indirect taxes, and in 1969 wholly through higher taxes. As a result, real personal disposable incomes and real personal consumption rose hardly at all between the collapse of the short-lived consumption boom of the first quarter of 1968 and the third quarter of 1969. It is not surprising that, with the rises in money incomes obtained in the last three quarters of 1968 and the first three quarters of 1969 almost entirely cancelled by higher prices, largely due to higher taxes, there should have been a great increase in the pressure for increases in money wage rates. The wage inflation of 1970 can therefore be regarded as a very unpleasant side-effect of the successful operation to expand exports in 1968 and 1969, after the devaluation of 1967.

A prolonged continuation of inflation at its present rate would inevitably bring a return of balance-of-payments difficulties, leading ultimately to a new devaluation and a further intensification of the inflation. Fortunately, however, the danger does not seem to be immediate. With the rise in labour costs in other industrial countries, most of them associated with a high demand for labour such as existed in the United Kingdom in 1964–66, the competitive advantage obtained by the 1967 devaluation seems so far to have been only partially eroded. With the help of a substantial improvement in the terms of trade in the second half of 1970, the current account surplus for that year was over £600 million. In 1971 this improvement in the terms of trade, due partly to a fall in the prices of some important raw materials, is helping to offset the effects of a faster rise in the volume of imports than in the volume of exports and the surplus on current account for the first five months seems to have been at a rate of about £500 million a year. But by 1972 the efforts of most other industrial countries to reduce the pressure of demand are likely to have slowed down their rises in wage costs, and unless by then there has also been a substantial slowing down in the UK, British producers are likely to find themselves at an increasing disadvantage both in the home and export markets. The government has therefore probably only a few months in which to get the situation under control.

III. THE ALTERNATIVES TO DIRECT RESTRAINT

Impressed by the earlier failures of the attempts made, in inappropriate conditions, to apply direct restraints to wage increases, the government is unwilling to use them now. In their place, two alternative policies have been proposed. The most obvious is an intensification of the policy of demand restraint. There are three types of demand to which restraint can be applied:

(i) personal consumption, which accounts for about 60 per cent of GNP at factor cost prices, and which can be restrained by further increases in taxation, either of personal incomes or consumption goods, by reductions in transfer payments from the government, or by charging, or increased charging, for free or subsidised government goods and services;

(ii) public sector expenditure on goods and services, which on both current and capital accounts absorbs about 28 per cent of GNP;

(iii) private sector investment (about 11 per cent of GNP), which could be restrained by restrictive monetary policy.

(i) Restraints on personal consumption

Of these, restraints on personal consumption affect by far the largest use of resources and offer the quickest and most powerful method of restraining demand, primarily for consumption goods and only secondarily for capital goods. It has, however, the disadvantage that it is likely, at least initially, to intensify the pressure for higher wages. The country would then be faced with the situation, envisaged as a hypothetical possibility on pages 16–17, where

'the combination of strong and ruthless unions with a government determined to prevent inflation at any cost will result in an unemployment level of 5 per cent, or even 10 per cent'.

It is difficult to believe that any government would to-day, except perhaps as a last resort, intentionally pursue a policy which would push unemployment up to well over a million.

(ii) Restrictions on public expenditure

To restrain demand by further restrictions on public expenditure on goods and services (apart from those which merely transfer part of the cost to the private sector, and have effects on demand similar to those of increased indirect taxes) would probably create a less immediately hostile reaction. Economies in public sector activities are, however, becoming increasingly difficult to find which do not imperil the defence of the country or of its inhabitants, or deprive them, now or in the near future, of urgently needed goods and services, such as hospitals, schools and prisons. If, nevertheless, public sector economies are carried far enough to have any appreciable effect on the rate of income rise, they must also involve additional redundancies and rising unemployment.

(iii) Monetary policy

The same considerations apply to a severely restrictive monetary policy, the impact effects of which are felt mainly by private sector investment. If such a policy can be enforced, in spite of the Treasury's need to fund nearly £2,000 million of debts maturing during 1971 and in spite of falling interest rates abroad, it will still further reduce the liquidity of private sector employers and make it more difficult for them to pay their debts. It is unlikely to make them less willing to meet pay claims—indeed, it may reduce their ability to afford strikes—but it will compel them to reduce expenditure on replenishing stocks and on improving capital equipment. A severe monetary restriction is therefore likely to be followed, not only by more insolvencies and rising unemployment, especially in capital goods industries, but also by a slowing-down of the rise in productivity and a reduction in the long-term rate of growth.

The very unpleasant and unpopular results of any major attempt to enforce further dis-inflation, whatever the means used, have prompted proposals for exactly the opposite policy—an attempt to buy off labour militancy by reducing personal and indirect taxes, thus accelerating the rise of disposable personal incomes and consumption and allowing output to rise faster than productive potential. Such a policy might well have some initial success, with a temporary slowing-down of the rise of prices and perhaps even of incomes. As soon, however, as the margin of unused potential had been substantially diminished, cost-push inflation would be re-inforced by demand inflation. At the same time, if not earlier, a rapid rise of imports would bring a return of balance-of-payments difficulties. The country would then be back in the familiar pattern of the 'stop-go' cycle.

IV. LONG-TERM AND SHORT-TERM MEASURES

Faced with the difficulty of fully applying any of the three possible policies for the control of inflation, the government has been placing most emphasis on long-term policies. While these, if successfully carried through and enforced, may bring more order into labour relations and perhaps some acceleration of the rise in productive potential, the time-scale for the measurement of their effects is in years rather than months. Meanwhile the government's short-term measures are borrowing some elements from each of the three possible anti-inflation policies, which it hopes will, in combination, bring a gradual slowing-down of the rise in employment incomes.

By the reduction of income tax announced in October 1970, the budget of March 1971 and the increase in retirement and other pensions announced for the autumn, the government is giving a substantial stimulus to personal consumption. As Table XXI shows, real personal incomes and consumption were already rising quite fast in the second half of 1970, with real disposable incomes nearly $4\frac{1}{2}$ per cent, and consumption nearly $3\frac{1}{2}$ per cent, higher than in the second half of 1969. The Treasury's projection, published in the 1971 *Financial Statement*,[1] estimates that the rise in consumption slowed down in the first half of 1971, as the result partly of price increases catching up on wage increases and partly of a rise in personal saving, possibly caused by fears of redundancies. With little rise in fixed investment and a heavy fall in investment in stocks, total output, as shown in Table XXII, was 0·5 per cent below that of the second half of 1970. As Table XVIII shows, this estimate implies that in the first half of 1971 the margin of unused potential has risen to 8·4 per cent. This is more than the equivalent of the first quarter's (seasonally corrected) unemployment percentage of 3 per cent, but closely comparable to the 3·4 per cent recorded in the second quarter. The Treasury also estimate that, without the additional stimulus to demand

[1] H of C Paper 330, HMSO, March, 1971.

given by the budget, total output would have risen by only 2 per cent between the first half of 1971 and the first half of 1972. This would have implied a rise in the margin of unused potential to over 9 per cent and in unemployment to about 850,000.

TABLE XXI

PERCENTAGE INCREASES IN PERSONAL INCOMES AND CONSUMPTION OVER CORRESPONDING PERIOD OF PREVIOUS YEAR, 1963–70

	Income from Employment	Total Personal Income before Tax	Disposable Personal Income	Prices of Consumer Goods and Services	Real Disposable Personal Incomes	Real Personal Consumption
1963	5·1	6·1	6·3	1·9	4·4	4·2
1964	8·3	8·1	7·5	3·2	4·1	3·5
1965	8·0	8·7	6·9	4·6	2·2	1·9
1966	7·0	6·7	5·9	3·8	2·1	2·1
1967	4·1	5·1	4·3	2·5	1·8	2·1
1968	6·8	7·4	6·3	4·5	1·7	2·3
1969	7·3	6·8	6·1	5·3	0·8	0·4
1970	12·1	10·4	9·2	5·5	3·5	2·9
Av. 1963–70	7·3	7·4	6·6	3·9	2·6	2·4
Year and quarter						
1969 I	6·3	6·8	5·9	6·0	—0·3	—3·1
II	7·3	6·6	6·0	5·0	1·0	2·4
III	7·0	6·3	5·9	5·0	0·8	1·2
IV	8·5	7·5	6·7	5·1	1·5	1·3
1970 I	9·3	7·2	6·0	4·6	1·3	2·4
II	11·6	10·8	9·2	5·0	3·9	2·5
III	13·8	11·8	10·7	5·9	4·6	3·6
IV	13·6	11·8	10·7	6·1	4·3	3·2
1971 I	11·8					1·6

Treasury Projection

1971	1st Half						3·3
	2nd Half						3·9
1972	1st Half						5·3

The measures announced in the budget, including the raising of social security benefits and contributions later in the year and a less restrictive monetary policy, are officially calculated to accelerate the rise of total output to just over 3 per cent, almost entirely by accelerating the rise of real disposable personal incomes and personal consumption; the effects, if any, on private sector investment of the reduction in corporation tax and of the moderate relaxation of monetary restraint are not likely to be seen before the second half of 1972. The rise in personal consumption is expected to accelerate from 1·1 per cent between the second half of 1970 and the first half of 1971 to 2·8 per cent between the first and second halves of 1971 and 2·5 per cent between the second half of 1971 and the first half of 1972. The rise of 5·3 per cent between the first half of 1971 and the first half of 1972, if achieved, will be the fastest for any year since the war. At the same time, the projected rise of 3·1 per cent in total output will leave the margin of unused potential and the level of unemployment almost unchanged. This combination of a very rapid expansion of personal consumption with a rise of total output little more than equal to that of productive potential will involve, as Table XXII shows, the devotion of the whole of the rise in output to personal consumption. This is not a policy which can be pursued for very long. While the present margin of unused potential may provide some reserve, soon after the middle of 1972 the rise of consumption will have to be slowed down to leave room for a much faster growth of investment and either a faster rise of exports or a slower rise of imports. These objectives are unlikely to be achieved unless the rise of employment incomes can be very substantially slowed down; but the government presumably feels that it is justified in taking risks in the hope that the rapid rise in real personal incomes and consumption will reduce the pressure behind the excessive wage demands.

'Unpleasant' alternatives

Besides expanding personal consumption while not allowing output to rise faster than productive potential, the government is trying to exert some measure of direct control on wage increases by bringing pressure to bear on public sector and, less effectively, on private sector employers, even at the risk of prolonged strikes. This combination of policies has a certain logic and there are signs in the indexes of wage-rates and earnings and in the estimates of employment incomes in the first quarter of 1971 that it is having some success. The alternative policies are all so unpleasant that the government is probably justified in postponing their use for as long as possible. If, however, there is no clear evidence of a substantial and maintained slowing-down of the rise in employment incomes by towards the end of 1971, it will have to consider what more positive action it can take.

There are three possible courses for further action: (a) to

attempt to conciliate labour by further tax reductions and a faster rise in consumption and output; (b) to enforce further deflation, either by fiscal or monetary means; and (c) to take some form of direct government action to restrain the rate of income rise.

(a) The margin of unused potential, after allowing for the change in the relationship (see pp. 72–3), is now consistent with a rise in employment incomes, in the absence of the use of monopoly power by labour, of between 4 and 5 per cent a year. It would therefore be unwise to give a further stimulus to the rise in consumption and output unless it was clear that they had risen, or were likely to rise, appreciably more slowly than the estimates given in the *Financial Statement*. There is a conflict of evidence about the level of output in the first quarter of 1971. As measured from the expenditure side, gross domestic product was a long way below the Treasury's estimate, while as measured from the output side it was in close agreement with it. While over long periods there is little difference between the two estimates, for quarterly movements the output index is usually preferable. Some confirmation of it can be found in the fact that unemployment in the second quarter was no higher than would be consistent with the Treasury's estimate of output in the first half of the year. Unless and until there is clear evidence that demand has fallen appreciably below the level which the Treasury assumed in drawing up their estimates, it would be unwise to introduce measures to expand it further, especially as most of the tax reductions introduced in the budget will become effective only in the second half of the year.

The uncertainty is even greater about the probable future rises in consumption and output. One of the main reasons for the slower rise of consumption in the first half of 1971, shown in the Treasury's estimate, was the slowing-down of the rise in earnings combined with an accelerated rise in prices reflecting the rising costs of several months earlier. If in the coming months earnings were to rise more slowly than the Treasury assumed in making its projection, the lagged rise in prices would mean that the rise in consumption, and probably in total output, would be less than estimated. Since the margin of unused potential seems now to be sufficient, in the absence of the use of monopoly power by labour, to keep the rise in employment incomes down to 5 per cent or less a year, it seems unnecessary to allow it, and with it unemployment, to rise further. If, therefore, the future rise in employment incomes turns out to be less than the Treasury has assumed, there would be a good case for sufficient tax reductions or other concessions to allow consumption and output to rise as rapidly as projected at the time of the budget. Official estimates indicate that the rise in employment incomes slowed down considerably in the first quarter of 1971. If this slower rate of increase is maintained in the second quarter, there will be a case for sufficient further tax reductions to allow the Treasury projections of consumption and output to be achieved, though not exceeded.

(b) The arguments against permitting spontaneous rises in the margin of potential and in unemployment apply equally to government action to force them higher. By now the inflation is almost wholly due to the use of labour monopoly power, and to attempt to cure it by a further severe dose of deflation would be as illogical as it would be to attempt to use general deflation as a cure for a producer's monopoly.

(c) If the rapid rise of employment incomes, after its check in the first quarter, is resumed later in the year, there remains the possibility of more direct government action to restrain it.

TABLE XXII

CHANGES IN NATIONAL EXPENDITURE AT 1963 PRICES (Seasonally Adjusted)

(As Percentages of Gross Domestic Product in Previous Half-Year)

| | Actual 1970 | | Treasury Projection 1971 | | 1972 |
	First Half	Second Half	First Half	Second Half	First Half
Consumption					
Personal	+0·7	+1·5	+0·7	+1·8	+1·6
Public Authorities	+0·2	—	+0·1	+0·1	+0·2
Total Consumption	+0·9	+1·5	+0·8	+1·9	+1·8
Fixed Investment					
Private Sector	—0·1	+0·2	+0·1	—0·1	+0·1
Public Sector	—	—	+0·1	+0·1	+0·1
Total Fixed Investment	—0·1	+0·2	+0·2	—	+0·2
Investment in Stocks	—0·5	+1·2	—1·3	+0·1	+0·3
Balance of Trade in Goods and Services					
Exports	+0·1	—	+0·5	+0·4	+0·2
Imports	+0·8	+0·6	+0·6	+0·6	+0·9
Balance of Trade	—0·7	—0·6	—0·1	—0·2	—0·7
Gross Domestic Product at Market Prices	—0·5	+2·3	—0·4	+1·8	+1·6
Adjustment to Factor Cost	—0·3	—0·2	—0·1	—0·2	—0·1
Gross Domestic Product at Factor Cost	—0·8	+2·1	—0·5	+1·6	+1·5

V. CONTROLS ON INCOMES AND PRICES?

The failure of earlier attempts at direct control of employment incomes has no bearing on the use of such a measure now. Previous attempts were designed to prevent increases in incomes caused by the excess demand for labour, and were therefore bound either to fail or to achieve only very temporary success. Their failure provides no indication of the probable result of a similar attempt made now, when the excess demand for labour has been eliminated and its sole purpose would be to restrain the use of monopoly power by labour. The only real difference between measures designed to restrain labour monopolies and other anti-monopoly measures is the much more stubborn difficulty of enforcement. It is true that employees as a whole would suffer only temporarily from measures which reduced the rise of money incomes. From Table XXI we see that the average annual rise in employment incomes between 1963 and 1970 was 7·3 per cent. From Table XX we see that, over the same period, the average annual rise in factor cost prices of gross domestic product was 3·8 per cent and in prices of consumption goods and services 3·9 per cent. The difference of about 3½ per cent between the average rate of rise of employment incomes and that of prices may have been somewhat exaggerated by the squeeze on business profits (the main reason for the slow rise of industrial and commercial investment), but we may safely put the future margin at about 3 per cent, which is the same as the estimated rate of growth of productive potential. If, therefore, the annual rise in employment incomes could be reduced to 5 per cent (which is probably a little above the rate of rise which, in the absence of the use of monopoly power by labour, would be consistent with the present margin of unused productive potential), the rise in prices of consumption goods and services could be expected to settle down, after a time-lag, at about 2 per cent a year. (Some tax reductions would be necessary to prevent a fall in consumption and output during the interval while the price rise was falling from over 2 per cent a quarter to less than a quarter of that rate.) Control of prices would therefore, in practice, be unnecessary. It would, however, probably be difficult to persuade employees that they would lose little or nothing by a slower rate of increase of money wages. It might, therefore, facilitate the acceptance of compulsory restriction of wage increases to, say, 5 per cent a year, if it were accompanied by a restriction of price increases to 2 per cent a year.

One difficulty which such a policy would encounter is that since, at the moment of its introduction, prices would not reflect past rises in costs, employers would be faced temporarily with a further erosion of profit margins. To offset this it would be necessary to offer substantial financial assistance, probably in the form of a reduction in taxes which increase business costs. It is important to note that the controls would not need to be more than temporary. Once the rates of increase in employment incomes and prices had settled down at their new levels, both compatible with the level of demand for labour, there seems no reason why they should not be maintained even after the withdrawal of government controls. The position would thus be quite different from that which has followed the withdrawal of controls imposed to restrain the effects of an excess demand for labour, when the rises in incomes and prices have immediately been resumed.

Tax on excessive wage increases?

If such a policy of direct control of wages and prices proves politically or administratively impracticable, there remains one other line of approach which seems worth exploring. Professor Sidney Weintraub, of the University of Pennsylvania, has suggested[1] that the resistance of private sector employers to excessive wage demands would be strengthened if they had to pay a progressive tax on wage and salary payments above a given rate of increase per employee (in the UK presumably about 5 per cent). Employers would be able to calculate in advance the total cost of accepting excessive wage demands, and in many cases would no doubt decide that it was likely to be larger than that of a strike. Professor Weintraub's suggestion could perhaps be strengthened if the government, besides taxing employers giving excessive wage increases, were to give financial assistance to firms suffering losses from strikes caused by refusals to grant increases above the given level. If all other measures seemed likely to fail, it might be worth while to explore the administrative practicability of such an approach.

[1] 'An Incomes Policy to Stop Inflation', *Lloyds Bank Review*, January 1971.

QUESTIONS FOR DISCUSSION

1. How far do you think that the objectives of full employment, rapid growth and stable prices are compatible?

2. What is the difference between cost inflation and demand inflation? At what periods since the war do you think that each of these has been important?

3. What is meant by 'productive potential'? How much has it increased in the United Kingdom in recent years, and why?

4. What is meant by the 'margin of unused productive potential'? What have been the relationships between this margin, the percentage of unemployment, the percentage of vacancies and the rate of rise in employment incomes, at different periods since 1952? How have the relationships changed, and why?

5. What is 'wage-drift'? When and why does it occur?

6. What is meant by an 'incomes policy'? Outline the methods used for carrying out such a policy in the United Kingdom in recent years and estimate their success. In what conditions, if any, is an 'incomes policy' likely to be successful?

7. To what causes do you attribute the rapid rise in money incomes in the United Kingdom (a) in 1967–69; (b) in 1969–71?

8. Why did the United Kingdom's balance of payments on current account worsen so much between 1958 and 1967, and improve in 1969–70?

9. What were the causes of the devaluation of sterling in November 1967, and what have been its effects?

10. What were the reasons for the Government's action to hold down personal consumption in 1968–69, and what has been its effects?

FURTHER READING

Bowers, J. K., Cheshire, P. C., and Webb, A. E.: 'The Change in the Relationship between Unemployment and Earnings Increases', National Institute *Economic Review*, November, 1970.

Dow, J. C. R. and Dicks-Mireaux, L. A.: 'The Determinants of Wage Inflation in the United Kingdom, 1946–56', *The Journal of the Royal Statistical Society*, Series A, Part 2, 1959. (Republished by National Institute of Economic and Social Research, Reprint Series No. 23.)

Dow, J. C. R.: *The Management of the British Economy, 1945–60*, National Institute of Economic and Social Research and Cambridge University Press, 1964.

Godley, W. A. H. and Shepherd, J. R.: 'Long-term Growth and Short-term Policy', National Institute *Economic Review*, August 1964.

Lipsey, R. G.: 'The Relation between Unemployment and the Rate of Change of Money Wage-rates in the United Kingdom, 1952–1957: a Further Analysis', *Economica*, February 1960.

Matthews, R. C. O.: 'Why Has Britain Had Full Employment Since the War?', *Economic Journal*, September 1968.

Paish, F. W.: *Studies in an Inflationary Economy*, Macmillan, 1962 (Chapter 17).
'*How the Economy Works, and Other Essays*', Macmillan, 1970 (Chapters 3–7).
'Business Cycles in Britain', *Lloyds Bank Review*, October 1970.

Pearce, D. W. and Taylor, J.: 'Spare Capacity: What Margin is Needed?', *Lloyds Bank Review*, July 1968.

Phelps, E. S.: 'Phillips Curves, Expectations of Inflation, and Optimal Unemployment Over Time', *Economica*, August 1967.

Phillips, A. W.: 'The Relation between Unemployment and the Rate of Money Wage-rates in the United Kingdom, 1861–1957', *Economica*, November 1958.

Romains, A.: 'Cost Inflation and Incomes Policies in Industrial Countries', *IMF Staff Papers*, March 1967.

Shepherd, J. R.: 'Productive Potential and the Demand for Labour', *Economic Trends*, August 1968.

Shultz, G. P. and Aliber, R. Z.: *Guidelines, Informal Controls, and the Marketplace*, University of Chicago Press, 1967.

London and Cambridge Economic Service: *The British Economy. Key Statistics 1900–1970*. The Times Newspapers Ltd., 1971.

Inflation, The Present Problem, OECD, December 1970.

OTHER IEA BOOKS ON EMPLOYMENT, INCOMES AND MONETARY POLICY

Hobart Paper 29
POLICY FOR INCOMES
F. W. PAISH and JOSSLEYN HENNESSY
1968 Fourth Edition *40p*

'The official unemployment figures are still high. If they can be taken at their face-value, there has been a jump in national productivity that justifies the optimism about the outlook that Professor Paish now feels. But the Treasury clearly suspects that they are not altogether comparable with those of the days before redundancy pay and wage-related unemployment benefit: and Professor Paish's optimism is in any case largely based on the assumption that no British government during the next few years will be able to risk the emergence of excess demand at home.' Leader in *Financial Times*

Hobart Paper 34
FULLER EMPLOYMENT?
M. J. FARRELL
1965 *40p*

'If you want to know how to live with inflation, or alternatively how to perish from it, you should study the brochure on *Fuller Employment?* by M. J. Farrell. His conclusions about the practicability of living with inflation make the advocates of a gentle 3 per cent per annum look like a set of timid reactionaries. . . .' *Sunday Times*

Hobart Paper 44
MONEY IN BOOM AND SLUMP
A. A. WALTERS
1970 Second Edition *40p*

'The words which form the text of this article are taken from a supplement to Professor A. A. Walters pamphlet. . . .

They sum up what I think will prove one of the most important discoveries in economics since the war in practical terms.' Economics Editor, *Guardian*

Hobart Paper 27
MONETARY POLICY FOR STABLE GROWTH
E. VICTOR MORGAN
1969 Third Edition *40p*

'Professor Morgan suggests that if only some of the steam could be let out of the economy by allowing the level of unemployment to rise fractionally from its present 1·4 per cent to 2 per cent, a greater measure of competition would generate more efficiency.
. . . He criticises the use of Bank rate to check the balance of payment crises. He argues that the net effect on reserves may be small, while the effects on the domestic economy of such measures are damaging to growth.' *Accountant*